Mastering "The Art of Retirement"

Stuart Gustafson

Mastering "The Art of Retirement"

CreateSpace Edition — November 2014

The material and information contained within this book are provided for informational purposes only. They are not meant to serve as legal advice (I am not an attorney), as investment advice (I am not a financial consultant), nor as tax advice (I am not a CPA or an accountant). They are a compilation of what people have told me as well as my own learnings over the years as I planned for, and looked forward to, the day when I would be able to "retire." If professional advice or other expert assistance is desired, you should consult with a competent advisor.

America's International Travel Expert is a

U.S. Registered Trademark of Stuart Gustafson Productions, LLC.

www.stuartgustafson.com

Also by Stuart Gustafson

Fiction:

Missing in Mexico

Sydney Murders--SOLVED!

Non-Fiction

Parables for Life in the 21st Century

Remembering our Parents . . . Stories and Sayings from Mom & Dad

PREFACE

Planning for retirement has changed! Hopefully, that is not a shock to you, although the changes themselves may be a shock to some people who thought that they'd "be taken care of" when they reached "retirement age. " We've seen companies eliminate pension plans; we've seen many a retirement program, 401(k) for example, lose value in the equity markets. There have been many instances where companies have filed for bankruptcy, or other forms of re-organization, and the pension plans or other retirement plans have taken a huge hit as part of the bargaining process. All of this is a way of saying that there are no guarantees in life and in retirement.

Well then, what are you supposed to do so you can "have a comfortable retirement"? Everyone's situation is different, although there are a lot of commonalities that can be used to your advantage. The purpose of this book is two-fold:

1. Make sure you know WHY YOU MUST prepare for your "golden years," and

2. Make sure you know HOW TO plan for and enjoy them!

I was fortunate to be able to take "Early Retirement" several years back when I was 59. I'd been with my current employer for only 13 ½years, but the opportunity to retire was too great to pass up. Would I have liked to have stayed on for a few more years to build up my savings? Of course; that would have been nice. But I also knew that the benefits I would receive by taking "the package" might not come along again.

So how was I able to retire at 59 when my original plan was to retire at 62 or later? Much of what I did to be able to retire is in this book. To me, there are two key aspects to retiring: the first is Financial, the second is everything else! This book is not about the financial aspects of retirement. I'm not a qualified to speak about financial planning, and there are tons of books already out there on that subject. This book is about the other aspects of retirement including why you need to start doing your "retirement activities" long before you actually retire.

Not everyone will be able to take advantage of everything I've included in the book, but I'm confident that if you do just one of the items that you'll be much better prepared for <u>your</u> retirement! Please let me know what you've done to master "The Art of Retirement.

Best wishes -- may your "Golden Years" truly shine!"

Stuart Gustafson

America's International Travel Expert®

Table of Contents

1 - INTRODUCTION to "The Art of Retirement" 1

2 - What I AM DOING now that I am "retired" 9

3 - Why you MUST START "retiring" 10 years in advance 16

4 - Uncovering your PASSION and unleashing its Power 25

5 - FINANCES are IMPORTANT, but they are not the only ingredient to a successful retirement 32

6 - How to AVOID some of the MISTAKES made by many retirees..37

7 - SIX DOCUMENTS that you must have 50

8 - VACATION SECRETS from a seasoned traveler 56

9 - FOUR PEOPLE you should know well, and vice versa 87

10 - Reference Materials 95

11 - THANK YOU 103

12 - About the Author 104

1 - INTRODUCTION to "The Art of Retirement"

Hi. My name is Stuart Gustafson, and I am in the group of tens of millions of Americans who are called "Baby Boomers." I was born in late 1947, so I was not among the first group of Boomers to reach 62 and thus become eligible to receive Social Security payments. My brother was born in January 1946, which meant that he was among the very first Baby Boomers to achieve that plateau.

In case you are curious, the picture on the cover is a picture of me at "my desk" in San José del Cabo in Baja California. Not a bad place to work is it? I was staying at Playa del Sol Los Cabos Resort (now part of the Bel Air Collection) for four weeks while I was completing the first edition of this book. I am an owner there, and I truly enjoyed the entire time I was there – the beach is clean; the waves are gentle, yet there is a world-class surfing beach a couple hundred yards away; everyone is friendly, both the staff and the vacationers. As I was considering where to go to complete writing this book on "The Art of Retirement," I could not think of a better place to go. As you look at that picture – don't you agree with me?

This book is written primarily for Baby Boomers. Why? Quite simply, January 2008 marked the date when the earliest of those Boomers reached the typical "retirement age" of 62. I know that age 62 is not the retirement age for everyone or for every line of work. The US armed services say you can retire, subject to a few limitations, upon reaching twenty years' of active duty service. For some that might mean age 38 if they joined the military at age 18. But for all those I know who retired from the military, they all went on to choose a second career. They were able to draw their retirement pay, but they took a new job, and many of them ended up retiring from their second job and receiving a retirement pension from that job. Smart planning!

1

And then there are those of us who go to work for a company where we expect to be able to retire at a certain age or after a set amount of years with that company. The expectation as you start out is that you will receive a comfortable monthly pension as a "thank you" from the company for the many years of service, dedication, and contribution to the company's growth and profits. This is the typical retirement benefit that one would expect to receive from an employer for having been employed for a certain length of time with them. Stay there "long enough" and you can retire (or, as put into other words, move into "retirement").

Recent turmoil in the worldwide business climate, combined with tougher economic situations within individual companies, has made some fairly wholesale changes to the retirement picture. Many companies have stopped their contribution to employee pension plans. Some have said that unless you were a certain age by a specific date, you would no longer be eligible for any retirement benefits – including the lifetime medical coverage that you were "promised" when you were hired. These are just a couple of the changes that are occurring that make "retirement" seem farther away and/or tighter from a budgetary viewpoint.

Retirement, however, is not just about staying with one particular employer long enough to receive retirement benefits. That can be one piece of it, and it could be a very important piece – but "retirement" is much more than that. Retirement should be the time in your life when you are mentally, physically, and financially able to do "whatever you want to do." That might be going fishing every day; it could be traveling to those places that you have only heard about on the Discovery Channel; or it could be going to visit your children and grandchildren on your own schedule. That sounds pretty good, doesn't it?

Most of us Baby Boomers were raised in a household where our parents would tell us of the struggles they had at work. Retirement to them was going

2

to be relaxing and doing things on "their schedule," not on the boss's schedule. Our parents were going to do the things that they were never able to do while they were working. They were going to get in the car and "just drive" to wherever they wanted to go. That all sounds so idyllic – it even sounds like some great material for some 1960's television programs – yet it was typically such a short-lived dream. Why? You will find out the specifics why later in this book, but basically our parents **had not** mastered "The Art of Retirement."

How could they have mastered "The Art of the Retirement"? They had never heard of it, so, of course, they could not master it. You have to realize that these people – the parents who brought us into the world and wanted us to have the things that were not a given to them – were so focused on making sure the family had a place to live, clean clothes to wear, food to eat, and an education so we could "go further" in life. They were much more focused on the basic elements of life, those things that we take for granted today. Let's not trivialize that because our generation is so much stronger because of the work ethic and the family ethic that our parents' generation had. Hopefully, some of that work ethic and family ethic has transferred down to our generation and then to the ones that follow.

Our parents' generation did not have an easy time of living and of making a living. Many of them served in World War 2, and some of them served in the Korean Conflict – and some in both – as did my dad. Their financial view of retirement consisted of a company and/or military pension plus a monthly Social Security check. Most of them had a paid-off house (they were raised being told to have minimal debt, meaning pay off the house as soon as possible) and they had no other outstanding debt (they did not believe in having other loans or charge card balances). They were now going to enjoy the "good life," something they "had earned" through their diligent and steadfast work. There is nothing wrong with that; they deserved it.

3

But something happened along the way that changed the way people looked at "retirement." As I said earlier, retirement should be the time in your life when you are mentally, physically, and financially able to do "whatever you want to do." So our parents' generation were financially ready for the next phase in their lives (retirement) because of their hard work and dedication, but many of them were not ready physically or mentally. Why do I say that?

Health care has come a long way in the twenty, thirty, or forty years' since "our parents" retired. The advances in medicine are allowing the current generation to stay healthier <u>while</u> <u>they</u> <u>are</u> <u>younger</u> as well as provide remedies for illnesses and other maladies that do arise. While these forms of remediation are also available for today's senior citizens, they did not have the better health care available to them when they were younger. Thus they are likely to have more medical problems affecting them than today's generation of upcoming retirees. Sure they might have a private insurance plan to go along with their Medicare coverage, but treating a problem is not the same as not having the problem in the first place. So now, rather than having a <u>preventative plan</u> against certain medical "problems," these people have a <u>maintenance plan</u> through prescription drugs. There is nothing wrong with taking prescription drugs, but wouldn't it be better to <u>not</u> have to take them rather than to <u>have</u> to take them?

I would be willing to bet that if you asked these same senior retirees about being "mentally prepared" to retire, they would either laugh in your face or ask you where you came up with that silly question. Of course they were mentally prepared. Why do you think they worked so hard all their lives – both at work and at home? It was so they would be able to retire and "enjoy the good life." Here is where the problem is – they did not know what the "good life" was going to be or was supposed to be. They just assumed that it <u>would</u> be a "good life." Whatever came along to them would, therefore, be "the good life" – the things that they had earned and now deserved. If you look at it from their point of view, you can't fault their logic; that is how they were brought up.

There is a saying, "When you fail to plan, you plan to fail." I am not saying that these people have failed in their retirement; just that they did not make optimal use of their retirement planning. Their planning consisted mostly of financial preparation – and we do know that financial planning is important – without much regard to what they were actually going to do during their golden years of retirement. They would do just what they wanted to do, right? Hmmm, what do you think? Do you think they are doing, or have done, everything that they would really like to do?

Do this simple survey – ask some senior citizens if there is anything they would still like to do. Some will say they have done everything they wanted to do – everything that was on their "bucket list." (By the way, I was promoting the idea of having a list of retirement activities before the movie "Bucket List" came out – you will find my template in Chapter 10 under "Retirement Activities.") Others will be honest with you, and say that there are things they would like to do if their health was better; if it was easier to walk; if their vision was better; if, if, if. "If" is the most self-debilitating two-letter word in the English language. Eliminate it from your vocabulary – change it to the phrase "I will."

The real question now is, "Do you want to be able to do everything that is available to you during your retirement?" I think you do, and the information in this book is going to help you do that. You have taken a great first step in achieving that goal by obtaining this book, and I'm extremely confident that you will benefit greatly from the information in this book.

With that said here is how I suggest that you take in and digest the information in the book. The book is written as a reference book that you can come back to at any time, which means that the chapters can be referred to "when needed." In essence, that implies that you could read them in any order the first time that you read the book. But I do not recommend doing that because I put the chapters in the book in a very orderly and logical manner. So if this is your first reading of the book, then I want you to read every chapter and every page in order from here through the end of the book. You will get most that is available from the book by reading the chapters in this order – I guarantee it.

What I AM DOING now that I am "retired" is not about ego or bragging. This chapter details the activities that I am now doing and how I prepared myself (and my family) for them. While you will not be able to copy them exactly, you will see what I did and what you can do to enjoy your retirement. [**TIP:** I tell you in this Chapter how the IRS puts money in my pocket to sit at a beach in Mexico and write books.]

Why you MUST START "retiring" 10 years in advance gives you the compelling reasons to begin your planning now. If you don't start planning early enough, you might end up like our parents' generation who just expected to be able to do whatever they wanted.

Uncovering your PASSION and unleashing its Power highlights how you can find the passion that is hiding inside of you, and how to use it to launch a second career or have it be a key activity during your retirement.

FINANCES are IMPORTANT, but they are not the only ingredient to a successful retirement reinforces the importance of financial readiness while also demonstrating the need for mental and physical readiness.

How to AVOID some of the MISTAKES made by many retirees reveals some of the pratfalls made by retirees and how you can avoid making the same mistakes. It is not a condemnation of the things they did, just information so you can make "eyes wide open" decisions in your retirement.

SIX DOCUMENTS that you must have outlines the documents that are very important to your life as a retiree. Don't assume right now that you know what they are because you just may be surprised when you read what they are and why you <u>must</u> <u>have</u> them.

VACATION SECRETS from a seasoned traveler reveals some of the travel tips that I have employed over the years as I have traveled literally around the world, and earned the US Registered Trademark *America's International Travel Expert*®. From getting a better seat on the airplane to going on a timeshare presentation – I will share what only a few of my closest friends have learned from me. You can tell by the length of this chapter that I love to travel.

FOUR PEOPLE you should know well, and vice versa tells you in no uncertain terms why these people become more important in your retirement years. You will find that there is actually a linkage between this and one other chapter in the book. This might be the hardest chapter for you to completely absorb, but do yourself and your family a favor – read this chapter in earnest and take it to heart.

Reference Materials contains listings of web sites and other items that you will find valuable. You may already know of some of these, but a gentle reminder of them should be okay. Look at these websites, and use them often!

Finally, when you find something in this book that was particularly helpful to you (saved you time, saved you money, made a vacation more enjoyable, etc.), please send an email to me telling me about your experience. I would love to be able to share with others how you benefited from the book – and I am confident that they would also appreciate them. Send your emails to stuart.a.gustafson@gmail.com.

Are you ready? Great – let's get going!!!

2 - What I AM DOING now that I am "retired"

Put simply, I am having fun now that I am retired. Let me put this into perspective for you.

I am sixty-six years old, and I have been retired for over seven years. I know that there are many people who have retired at a younger age than this. But I am not the super-millionaire who made his riches through some internet company that was sold for gobs of money to a high-capitalization company. There's nothing wrong with that if you can do it. Even though that is the type of "cash out" that gets the headlines, it is actually a rarity. Much more common is the situation where a person has worked for a company, or has owned a small business, and has finally gotten to the point in his or her life where he (or she) can "call it quits" and retire.

That pretty much sums up my situation. I worked for six companies after I received my degree in Mathematics from San Diego State University (not counting the stint attempting to peddle life insurance to college students). Along the way I also earned an MBA from the University of San Diego. The longest that I worked for any of these companies was thirteen and one-half years; the shortest was eight months. So I certainly do not fit into the typical mold of someone who works for a company for twenty to thirty years and then retires with a very nice pension check being deposited monthly into the checking account.

But the beauty of this is that if I am able to retire before my "Social Security retirement age" without having followed the typical working path to retirement, then so can you. Does that pique your interest? We will go more into that in the next chapter.

What am I doing now that I am retired? Aside from planning a lot of travel; tending our small garden, and enjoying wearing shorts and a Hawaiian shirt during the summer months, I am doing a lot of writing. My co-author (Robyn Freedman Spizman – www.robynspizman.com) and I received a multi-book contract for our "Questions to Bring You Closer" series of books, nationally published by Adams Media. Our first book, *Questions to Bring You Closer to Dad* came out in April 2007, and it was a big hit for Father's Day. I had many radio interviews all across the country and in Canada, and I had five local TV interviews. There were also quite a few e-articles as well as articles in print, including one national magazine with 4.5 million members. Given that it was just the first book in the series, we were excited with the reception the book received. As an author, it is not just about sales (although it is better to have more sales than fewer sales). I received some marvelous emails from people who bought the book and used it to re-connect with their Dad – that is what drives an author to write more books!

The second book *Questions to Bring You Closer to Mom* was released in April 2008 in time for Mothers' Day – early feedback on it was that it was also well received because of the way it helps the readers see and appreciate a different side of Mom. I have a copy that I took with me when I visited my Mom. She recently passed away at age 94, but the last years weren't wasted because we had times together to talk. I would ask her some of the questions in the book, and I would occasionally be surprised by her answers! I am building a life-long keepsake that will mean so much to me and my family in later years.

Questions to Bring You Closer to Grandma & Grandpa was released in August 2008. This book takes a different look at grandparents and how you get to really know them. I never really knew my grandparents so this book really was emotional for me.

I worked with Joe Prin, a local remodeling expert, on a series of books – the first one is "I Want a New House." It's been out for five years now, and it was fun working on it. Joe hosts an hourly radio show every weekend (for the past 25 years), and he has a ton of knowledge on home repairs that he shares with his listeners every weekend. If you have any questions about home repair projects, check out Joe's website at www.JoePrin.com.

My wife and I took two mini-vacations in the first three months' of my retirement. This might not sound like much, but for someone who was on the road a lot while working, being able to head out of town with my wife is a wonderful change. These trips were short by choice, not by necessity. We also spent our "normal" two weeks in Cabo San Lucas, Baja California, Mexico – we love going there in February each year, and we now spend four, or more, weeks each year down there. We are tired of the winter here in Boise by then, and the temperatures in Cabo are in the mid-70's. That is good enough for us at that time of the year.

Prior to our regular February trip to Mexico, I took my then 90-year-old Mom down to Australia where we went on a 14-day cruise of New Zealand. The idea for this trip came about during a dinner at our house right after I retired in 2007. Mom lived only 5 blocks from our house, and she was looking through my old passport after dinner. The passport was full and I had to get a new one. After looking through it, she said there were a few places where I had been that she still wanted to visit, but that New Zealand was tops on her list. So I told her, "Then we'll go there." So we went there. We didn't dance the night away on the Lido Deck, but we did have a great time on the trip. Even though we had some long flights (15-hour non-stop from San Francisco to Sydney, Australia – going and returning), Mom did really well. I am beginning to understand why seniors like to go on cruises. You unpack one time; there is fantastic service onboard; the food is marvelous; everyone has a great time. That sure sounds like a great way to travel to me!

Oh, I left out the 4-week "personal retreat" that I took to San José del Cabo at the tip of Mexico's Baja California. You already know that my wife and I go to Cabo San Lucas for at least two weeks in February each year. But this 4-week trip was more of a "retirement gift" to myself, and it was not just party time. I spent most of the time writing – I am working on more books than I mentioned at the beginning of this chapter. Plus, my wife did come down to Cabo for a part of the time while I was there. We were able to explore the town of San José del Cabo with a much more relaxed feeling than when we have been there before. It was so wonderful; no pressures and no calendars to consult. Oh, before I forget, here is the best part about that 4-week trip. While I was writing in Mexico, **the IRS was putting money in my pocket every day** that I was working there! How is that? A little-known fact is that the IRS publishes per diem rates for allowable expenses in both the Continental US and outside the US. My tax advisor says this was a legitimate business trip, and therefore I was entitled to claim these expenses. You will want to check with your tax advisor to see if this applies in your situation. I have provided the website addresses for these per diem rates in Chapter 10 (Reference Materials).

In June 2008 my son and I went to San Diego, California, so we could attend the US Open Golf Tournament. One of the items on my "Retirement Activities" list has been to attend at least one "major" event in golf and tennis. The US Open was being played at Torrey Pines Golf Club in La Jolla, a most spectacular course. My son played that course in the Junior World Championships when he was 17, so going back there held an extra special memory for him. We were at the course for all eight days (three days of practice rounds; four tournament rounds, and the magnificent 19-hole playoff on Monday after Father's Day). We had a great time at the course, plus it gave us some time together to just talk.

What else have I been doing? I have an extensive CD collection of classical music as well as the **complete works** of Wolfgang Amadeus Mozart – that Mozart set alone is 171 CD's. As you can see, I really do love classical music. I've collaborated with a gifted musician on a composition that we are still hoping to have premiered "soon." We have very high expectations for the piece that is based on one of the most well-known pieces of classical music. Regardless of how it is received, it has been such a tremendous joy to work on this composition because it has allowed me to express some inner feelings that are only shown through music.

The only thing that I have not been able to do much of is to paint. Yes, I have done some touch-up painting on the house trim. What I meant is that I have not spent a whole lot of time doing expressionistic painting. My studio has 10 paintings that are depictions from photos that I took on our 2006 trip to Italy, and I've also created some "Escher-type" paintings. Gee, I feel that I am busier now than when I was working! But am I complaining – not at all!!!

I have flown to a lot of places; I've received my Million-Mile Flyer card from United Airlines; my wife and I took a four-week trip to Europe that included a 19-day cruise from Barcelona through the Suez Canal to Dubai. I've published two travel-based mystery novels, and more are on the way. I've also been invited to speak on lots of cruise ships; what do I speak about? Travel, of course!

By now you might be asking yourself, "Why is he telling me all this? That's nice that he is able to do lots of travel and write books and compose music, but how does that relate to me?" I hope you **are asking** that question because that means that you want to know what **you can do** to get ready for your own retirement. I am doing these things because I want to do them, because I have planned for them, and because I want you to know how to plan to be ready to do what you want to do "in retirement."

There is one more reason why I am focusing so much on travel so soon after retirement. I have seen many people who said they wanted to go places after they retired, but they waited to do it. Then, once they were ready (perhaps mentally or financially), there were not physically able to go on those trips. I don't expect that to happen to me at any point in the near future, but those people probably didn't expect it to happen to them. After all, I am "only" sixty-six and in good health. But we all know that health conditions can change in a moment's notice. I want to make sure that I do not wait to travel until it is too late to travel. You can agree with my logic or you can disagree with it. Either way is okay with me – I just want you to know the thought processes that I have used in making my decisions.

On the home front, I do prepare more dinners than I used to do, and I clean up the dishes after every meal. My wife finally retired because she realized that she couldn't work even part-time and still commit to going to all the places that were available to us. I have not yet gotten into the habit of vacuuming the carpets on a regular basis, but I do keep the kitchen dishes washed and put away. I make the bed every day (we used to have the rule that last person out of the bed would have to make it – I guess that would fall to me anyway these days!), and I have actually gotten better on putting my clothes away in the closet or into the hamper.

Here is the bottom line to all of this. Now that I am retired I am able to do the things that I enjoy doing; I am able to do the things that I want to do, and I am able to do the things that are good for our marriage. We try to have an annual garden with tomatoes, peppers, pole beans, and cucumbers. I like to incorporate our home-grown vegetables into the meals that I prepare; certainly a tomato will be included once they start ripening. My guess is that our tomatoes have a dollar cost that is higher than the cost of the tomatoes in the grocery store, but ours taste much better than "store bought" tomatoes. I still have some more learning and "training" before I will consider myself to be a good household meal preparer, but I am making progress. The best part of all of this is that my wife and I are both enjoying these transitions from working into retirement.

So how does all of this relate to you? After all, what I am doing is much less relevant to you than what you can be doing in your retirement. I am doing things that I want to do, and I am doing them pretty much on my schedule (book publishers have a different view of it, but that's okay). Wouldn't you like to be doing the things that you really want to do? And wouldn't you like to be doing them without the hassles of a boss or employer who seems to also have control over your spare time? Before you dispute that, think of your last two or three vacations? Did you check voicemail or e-mail while you were away from the office? Were you truly "on vacation" the moment you left work, and did you avoid thinking about work (or worse yet, doing work) until you were actually back on the job? Been there, done that.

I haven't thought about work since I retired, and I don't consider what I do to be work. You can do that too once you have mastered "The Art of Retirement." You are on your way to doing that now that you are reading this book. I am confident that you will succeed and launch yourself into a retirement that surpasses your current expectations. I have found that, even though I did a lot of planning and preparation for retirement, it still takes a lot of practice to truly enjoy your retirement. I am now into my eighth year of retirement, and I am continuing to work on that piece of it right now – how to truly enjoy my own retirement.

3 - Why you MUST START "retiring" 10 years in advance

For most people, "retirement" seems far off – many, many years into the future. It's something that is dreamed of; most people have certainly even talked about. But actually getting to retirement is not a reality that most people can grasp. The truth is that retirement will arrive faster than most people think it will arrive. Why is that? When you are not focused on an event occurring, you are obviously not thinking about it. You know it will eventually happen, but it will seem like a surprise. Don't get me wrong, surprises are nice (did you ever have a surprise birthday party when you were young?), but something as important as retirement should <u>not</u> come as a surprise to you!

When I tell people that they must start their retirement ten years before the actual retirement date, the typical response is "Huh?" They don't understand what I mean when I tell them to "start their retirement," so I then explain it to them; which is what I am going to do for you now.

Starting your retirement is not as much about a certain date as it is about your state of mind and the activities in which you are currently engaged and the ones that you <u>think</u> you will want to do when you retire. The emphasis on "think" is intentional because <u>you</u> <u>don't</u> <u>know</u> what you will do when you retire; you only think you know what you will do. Maybe the first couple of years will play out as you "think" they will; after that, however, could be really different.

I know this might be radical thinking for some people. After all, the traditional school of thought is that retirement is about getting to a time in which you have met some number of "years of service." That requirement typically does exist in order for you to be able to receive "retirement benefits" from an employer. But your retirement is not going to be just about meeting some quantitative criteria; your retirement will be concentrated on the activities that you want to do, and the accomplishments that you want to see occur. In other words, your retirement is **not** going to be a passive one where you do nothing but "sit around" all day long.

All of us have different activities that we want to pursue in our lives. This is true whether we are single and forty, a young couple in our twenties, or if we have "entered retirement." This is not to say that our activities will remain the same throughout the different stages in our life. Some will definitely stay with us, but others will change as we change. And we will also take on new activities as we discover them or as they are introduced to us. The next chapter (Uncovering your PASSION and unleashing its Power) will focus on a very specific aspect of retirement activities – that special "calling" that many of us have during retirement or that we use to launch a second career. Sometimes these new activities that we did not even think about before retirement become a central part of our everyday life.

If I had not started retiring about ten years ago, my wife and I would not have been ready to accept the early retirement offer from my company because we would not have been ready both mentally and financially. What I mean by starting my "retiring" years ago is that we started to act as if we were retired and we did the things we were planning to do once we actually did retire. This means that we started to live financially as if we were retired; we did the activities that we wanted to do when we retired, and we acted and responded mentally as if we were already retired. By doing these things, the actual retirement date would then be just another day on the calendar – it would not be a major life-changing event just because we had formally retired. We had observed some of the errors that many retirees made, and we did not want to repeat them (not that we have not made our own mistakes along the way to retirement). Some of those errors are discussed in a later chapter (How to AVOID some of the MISTAKES made by many retirees).

From a financial point of view, we had already decided that we would enter retirement with no debt. Our house would be paid off, and we would have no car payments or outstanding credit card bills. You do not have to agree with our plan, but you need to have a plan. There are people who say they don't care about having a paid-off house – they can make more money "in the market" than their mortgage is costing them. That's okay if they want to make that conscious choice – it is just not our choice. We also had defined a certain level of annual income that we would need for our retirement life style and for routine expenses (food, utilities, taxes, etc.).

By saying that we wanted to have no debts as we entered retirement, we had set out a plan that would allow us to achieve that. But our plan was based on my retiring somewhere from September 2008 to January 2009. When the company announced an early retirement plan in February of 2007 (with an effective "retirement date" of May 31, 2007), we had to re-assess our plan and see if we could still achieve it. The good news is that we felt that we could have our obligations paid off by exercising some of the company stock options that I held. Our tax accountant advised us to not exercise those options until 2008 so that we would be in a lower tax bracket than if they were exercised in 2007 (that advice saved us thousands of dollars in taxes alone). We then had to consider our living expenses for the remainder of 2007 and for most of 2008 since I would not be receiving a paycheck after May 31, 2007. By using some of our savings combined with my wife's salary, we saw that we would be able to "make it," although it meant that we would not be able to do the same amount of travel and additional entertainment as we had done in the past.

Once we saw that "it would work," the decision to take the early retirement was done. I applied for and got it, and we have not regretted that decision at all. Sure, our bank accounts might have been a little larger had I waited until my "planned retirement time." But our mental accounts are much fuller now that I am free to do what I want to do. And I know for certain that we would not have been able to make the same decision (for me to retire early) if we had not started retiring about ten years ago. Maybe you don't need ten years, or eight years, or even five years to get to the same place as we did. That's okay. Pick a timeframe that will work for you, and then "start retiring."

Another thing we did was to decide on places where we liked to vacation. We have always liked sunny beach areas; perhaps that is because we lived for over twenty years in the San Diego area of Southern California. We also like metropolitan areas such as New York City and Paris, France, but those are not places where we felt we would want to visit on a frequent basis (such as every two or three years). Knowing that we liked to vacation in these warm areas that have nice beaches, we decided to acquire some timeshare properties in these locations. This gave us the chance to try them out before retiring, and we were also able to afford them while we were still working. If we had waited until after "retirement," we might not have felt that we could afford to then purchase them. We have had no regrets about the timeshares – in fact, I spent four weeks at one of them on a personal "writing retreat" just a few months following my "actual retirement." I will write more about timeshares, etc., later in the book (VACATION SECRETS from a seasoned traveler).

The other big piece of the financial picture in retirement is your annual budget. While most of us have generally been accustomed to working with budgets or financial projections on a monthly basis, we have to reset that thinking once we get to retirement. The primary reason for this is that some portion of your income will now be coming in on a quarterly, semi-annual, or even an annual basis. If you have an annuity that pays you interest every quarter, or if you have a Certificate of Deposit (CD) that pays interest every twelve months, you cannot spend that money until it is deposited into your account. So unlike that monthly or semi-monthly paycheck that you gave up when you retired, your annuities and CDs are now giving you an income on a less frequent basis.

At the end of the year, it is still the same amount of money whether you get it once a month or once every six months. The key is that you must plan for your regular expenses out of the <u>previous</u> annuity or CD interest payment, <u>not the future one</u>. Many of you who are in a sales role are used to this thinking because a portion of your income (sometimes, a very significant portion of that income) is received on a quarterly or other basis that is not monthly. I have never heard of a mortgage company that would accept an IOU based on your future commission check. No, they want their payment now; which means that you have to adjust your cash flow planning to account for the expenses that come in before the income does. This situation becomes even more accentuated in your retirement. You might have a monthly pension payment as well as a Social Security check that comes in once a month, but most people will also have other investments and sources of income that are not paid out on a monthly basis. Thus the reason to take a 12-month look at your expenses and your income is so that you can make sure that you have the necessary funds available when each expense comes due – whether it is once a month; once every three months; once a year; or even just once, period.

So far in talking about retiring ten years early, I have talked mostly about the financial picture that you want to get into. Again, the main reason you want to begin your financial retiring before your "actual retirement date" is so that you will become accustomed to that part of your retirement and feel comfortable with it. It also allows you to be able to make changes should you decide that the financial picture that you see yourself in is not the one that you want, or truly feel that you can do. Remember, the primary point of **Mastering "The Art of Retirement"** is to ensure that you do not encounter any unpleasant surprises in your retirement. Starting your retiring ten years in advance should allow you to see any of those surprises, and then deal with them while you still have enough time to make the necessary adjustments to either your plans or to your financial situation – or both.

Even though the financial part of retirement is a significant piece of it, there is more to retirement than just money. Okay, I can wait until you stop laughing. Sure, the more money you have, the earlier that you might be able to retire. Notice that I said "might be able to" – and emphasis should be on *might*. Let me repeat that phrase with some additional emphasis: There is MUCH MORE to retirement than money. Money certainly plays an important role in your retirement (believe me, it plays an important part in my retirement!), but it is not the only piece of it.

Another very important piece of your retirement is your health. When was the last time that you had a complete physical examination by your doctor? By complete, I mean to include all those exams that we typically do not like to talk about – the colonoscopy; the breast exam; the prostate exam; the blood sugar test if there is a history of diabetes in the family. Get the point? This stuff is not something to kid about. Do you want to make grandiose retirement plans only to find out that your health condition will not allow you to move forward with those plans? I have seen many people who were going to do so many things in retirement – only to have their health issues preclude their doing them.

There are two ways to look at this. One of them – the preferred one – is to ensure that you are doing your regular health checks so that you and your health professionals can address any issues that might arise. The other approach (and there might actually be even more than one more) is to do the things that you want to do before "it is too late." I do not prefer this one, but it is an understandable position if you feel that your health situation warrants this approach. I have a neighbor who is about five years older than I am, and we both coached Under-12 Boys soccer at the same time – my son played against his son in a few games. I had a conversation with him recently, and he revealed that his family history is that the males do not live past seventy-five. He may beat that, but then, history might tell him that his time is up in about five years from now. Based on that, I expect him to live his life as if it is going to end at 75. It's not the approach I would take, but I can see why he would.

Think about it – what would you do if your life expectancy was only five years after your retirement? Would you do whatever you could to extend that time beyond five years, or would you live those five years to the fullest and with no regrets? Would your children say that you were "spending their inheritance"? Mortality does have a way of altering the way that we think and the way that we do certain things.

Getting back to discussing your health as you begin your retiring ten years early, you <u>must</u> schedule annual checkups and follow up visits. If you are married or have a significant other, here is a "gift" that you can give to that special person in your life. When it is his or her birthday, get a card (it does not matter if it is funny or serious) and write the following inside it: "My gift to you this year is the promise that I will have regular doctor visits so that we can enjoy all the activities that we have talked about and planned to do." Pay special attention to his or her eyes as the card is read. What you have told him or her is that you will manage your health so that all the future plans that you have made together will not be stopped because of your failing to take care of yourself health-wise. The amazing thing about that gift is that it really doesn't cost you anything – it can actually save you money in the long run.

Another benefit of having your regular checkups in the years before "they really become critical" is that they become a regular habit for you. They are no longer one of those dreaded doctor visits that you will do anything you can to avoid. When I say "doctor visits," I am also referring to dental visits and your vision checks as well. I do not have the statistics for serious diseases that are initiated by problems with the gums, but I do know that gum disease is preventable. But to prevent it, you have to know about it, which means that you must have your regular dental checkups, including teeth cleaning, etc.

The same holds true for regular visits to your eye doctor. Scheduling your annual vision checkup is not just a matter of checking to see if your prescription for glasses (or contact lenses) has changed. My eye professional also checks my eyes for glaucoma and other diseases such as the onset of macular degeneration. I consider my visits to my eye doctor as an investment in the future that my wife and I plan to have together for a very long time. I hope that you will view all of your medical visits as a way of ensuring that your future and your retirement will be as healthy and as wonderful as you have planned them to be.

There are links to some "health" websites in Reference Materials chapter – check them out to see what other things you can be doing to ensure your retirement is a healthy one. Even if you are a health professional yourself, you know that you can't know all you need to know about general medical health, about your teeth, and about your eyes. I put those sites there to help you; I hope you use them.

In summary, starting your retiring ten years in advance is a way for you to transition into that golden time of your life when you are entitled to enjoy all the things that you have earned and that you now deserve. While it's true that you might leave your job on one day (your "retirement date"), and then "be retired" on the next day – that does not mean that your life has to change that instantly like the flip of a light switch. Wouldn't you rather gradually move into retirement so that you know what to expect? I think you do or you probably would not be reading this book.

You will also find out during this transition phase that there are some things that you thought you would like to do when you retired, but you actually don't like them as much as you thought you might, or you don't want to do them. That is okay – in fact it is far better to find that out before you retire than after. What you will actually discover when you do officially retire is that it does not seem like much of a change for you; and that is the whole idea. Your retirement should be a gentle transition from one phase in your life to the next. It should not a drastic change, and it won't be when you start "retiring" ten years in advance.

4 - Uncovering your PASSION and unleashing its Power

If I had not begun my "retiring" process many years ago, I would not be doing many of the activities that I am doing today. Why? The simple answer is that I would have expected that retirement would "show" me what I should be doing, rather than my entering retirement and doing the things that I wanted to do. A key factor in this difference is that my starting to retire years earlier allowed me to focus on what it was that I wanted to do once I actually retired. There was not this huge "Eureka!" moment; instead, it was a gradual process that eventually pointed out what I really wanted to do. And what was that?

What became apparent to me was that I enjoyed writing and helping other people through what I wrote. When this came to me – when it became apparent that it was very important to me – this is what I called "Uncovering the Passion." What was it that I wanted to do that would allow me to express my feelings, and that I would devote hours and hours to doing regardless of the lateness of the evening or the early morning of the day? That passion to me was expressing my feelings and knowledge through the written word. I had always enjoyed "dabbling" in writing, and my first published book *Parables for Life in the 21st Century* was a product of a span of twenty years' of writing. I have not done any polling, but I am going to guess that you cannot be too successful at writing if it takes you twenty years to get each book written.

Fortunately for me it didn't take that long to get the next book published. While my first book was self-published (faster, but costing me more up-front money), the next book was published by Adams Media, a traditional publisher out of Massachusetts. This book, *Questions to Bring You Closer to Dad*, was written with a fantastic co-author, and was released on a national basis three months before Father's Day in 2007. I have seen it for sale on at least four continents, although they all seem to be an English version of the book. Without going into too much detail, my co-author and I have a multi-book contract for a series of these books; there are links for the books online in the Reference Materials chapter. The second book in the series *Questions to Bring You Closer to Mom* was released in April 2008 (in time for Mother's Day), and the third book was released a year later – *Questions to Bring You Closer to Grandma & Grandpa*. As you can see, there is a pattern to the titles – it is an exciting series, and you can find the books on Amazon.

Going back to my first book, it had always been my plan to have a **Parables for Life in the 21st Century** series of books. If you ever pick up a copy of the book *Parables for Life in the 21st Century*, you will notice a numeral '1' on the spine – the first in the series. That was all a part of the original planning. That series is now becoming a reality (www.parablesforlife.com) with the second book (*Parables for Life as a 21st Century Teenager*) being about 70% complete. The stories in this book are being written by teenagers, and for teenagers. I am hoping to use that model to have stories submitted for books – stories that written by people who would actually by the book (teenagers write stories for the *Teenager* book; parents write stories for *Parables for Life as a 21st Century Parent*, etc.). If you think you have any interest in writing a story to be published in this series, please get all the details at www.parablesforlife.com.

As I mentioned in Chapter 2, I also worked with a local remodeling expert on writing a book series – the first book is called *I Want a New House*. It's fun working with Joe, and it will be a really educational series of books. Joe has also done a great job of remodeling our bathrooms to be more functional!

I've also written several travel-based mystery novels that are set in locations where I've spent a lot of time. Going somewhere that you enjoy is great; writing about them truly adds to the pleasure. My first novel, *Missing in Mexico*, is set in Los Cabos, where we've been going every year since 2003.

The next one, *Sydney Murders SOLVED!*, is set in Australia's largest city, and I think you'd enjoy reading about the security flaw in the Sydney Harbour Bridge that I reveal in the book. The third one is set on a cruise ship in the Mediterranean, a setting that is a natural based on my speaking on many cruise ships. I have other book "ideas" that are in various stages of thought and development; I am certainly not lacking any ideas!

The point of my telling you about these books is that I was working on some of them (both the writing and the process of getting them published) concurrent with my working full-time prior to my retirement. My casual attraction to writing struck a harmonious chord within me and I realized that this was a passion that had been inside of me for a long time. Thus my own passion had been uncovered and it was now up to me to make the most of it and unleash its power. Now that my time is "my time," I can channel that passion to meet my own desires. I have been able to unleash the power of writing and let it find its own path – just as water will find its own way down a mountain. The path that my writing has taken me is to provide books that will inspire and help other people, while other books will be read purely for enjoyment. Sure, I can make some money along the way, but I am not doing it for the money. I have no visions of hitting the *New York Times* Bestseller list. I just want people to have their own lives enriched by what I have written.

The reason that it is vital to uncover your passion is that you do not want to enter retirement without any driving force behind what you do. In other words, if your idea of retirement is sitting around all day perhaps drinking coffee or iced tea (or something stronger!), then you are doomed to an early exit not only from retirement, but from life itself. You must have something that gives you the reason to stay active both mentally and physically or you will find that your body and your mind are quickly decaying.

You might be saying, "But wait. I have worked all my life. I want to retire so that I can take it easy." There is nothing wrong with taking it easy and enjoying a quieter schedule once you are retired. The passion – that driving force that you discover that motivates you each and every day – might be something like reading the classics from literature. It could be helping out at a downtown soup kitchen serving meals once a month (or once a week) to the homeless. Perhaps it is spending a couple hours each week reading to young children at the library – this not only enhances their minds, but it can also give their parents a much-needed short break. Maybe it is learning the different species of birds in your area, and marking when and where you saw them. A lot of retirees want to live in a sunny climate where they can play golf any day of their choice.

I have a friend who decided that he really wanted to teach High School mathematics. I have an undergraduate degree in math, so I immediately thought he was crazy to want to do this. But he said he had always wanted to teach math – to use his innate skills at logic – to help students learn the basics underlying algebra, geometry, etc. He was willing to leave a high-paying high-technology job to pursue this passion that he had. He was so immensely energized in his pursuit of this uncovered passion that he was not going to let anything get in his way. Ron found his passion, and now its tremendous power had been unleashed. He is now starting on a second career; one that he feels is just as satisfying and stimulating as his first one. And the school is only a ten-minute walk from his house! So he's doing what he wants to do; he gets daily exercise by walking to and from school, and he does not have to drive.

So what are some things that you might want to do, what might be your passion? Here are some suggestions; don't worry if these don't appeal to you right now. Think about them, and then let your mind just work on its own. Perhaps your brain will kick out some other ideas that align more closely with you.

Write – you have already read (perhaps even more than you cared to read) about my writing and how much I enjoy it. You don't have to write just to get published. Maybe you write in a journal once a day or once a week as a way of reflecting on what you've done and how you've felt. Perhaps you start writing some poetry and do readings at local bookstores or coffee shops.

Study a language – have you ever traveled to a different country and wished you knew *their* language so you could converse more easily? Well, now you have the time to do it. Many local community education programs offer beginning language programs. This is an easy way to get started; the programs are typically inexpensive, and you can meet some other people who share a similar goal. Now when you go back to that country, you will be able to do more exploring and blending in with the locals because you are speaking their language. There are more formal language programs, but the community education method will probably be the cheapest (checking out tape/CD programs from the library will be the cheapest – that's another way to do it).

Go back to school – did you ever say, "When I have some free time I will finish my degree"? Or maybe you already have the degree(s), but you would like to take some classes in cooking, pottery, home accounting, gardening, belly dancing, etc., etc. The possibilities are endless here. Whether it is a single class or an entire program – now you have the time! Again, look into the community education programs first. You can also look up local chapters of the particular organization that would "host" that activity.

Take up painting or another craft – do you have a hobby that you wish you had more time to enjoy? You already know that writing is mine, but I also dabble a little in painting. There is a lady at our church, Bertha, who took up water painting about seven years' ago – in her late seventies. Her work is marvelous. She has entered several juried

29

competitions and won some prizes. Bertha has also sold her paintings as well as cards made from them. What is your hobby – or what would you like to take up – that would give you a lot of enjoyment as you do it? How do you start? You watch the paper for notices about "beginner classes" or you call the local watercolor society. Who knows – maybe you could become another Grandma Moses? If nothing else, you will have some original artwork that you can give away as presents. Maybe it's not painting; perhaps it's knitting, cabinetry, gardening, or auto mechanics. Whatever it is, get started on it – you could find a whole dimension of your life that you didn't know existed.

Volunteer – could you spare a couple hours each week helping out somewhere? There are so many possibilities where you can volunteer your time and your talents: school, hospital, nursing home, library, food bank, soup kitchen, youth center, senior center, non-profit agency, community events, local theatre company, ... CAUTION: it is easy to get over-committed, so it is up to you to protect your time and don't volunteer for more than you can handle. It is better to start out slowly – you can always add time later on. Don't worry, you won't be told, "No we don't want any more of your free time."

Second career – depending on your age and other factors, now you can begin a new full-time or even a part-time second career. Even if it is not a "career" in the same sense as the one you retired from, it can be a new paying job that is a whole new path for you. For example, Ron left a finance career in high-tech to become a math teacher. I have known well-educated people who have become school bus drivers. The job has significant responsibility, but the job was always "Done" at the end of the day, and there were no conference calls or weekend work. You might even take your hobby and turn it into a business.

30

Perhaps you rent a kiosk at the shopping center to sell your crafts. Or maybe you sell those same crafts to already established retails stores.

Uncovering your passion can be a significant factor if you are changing careers. This re-focus of purpose will give you more energy and drive than all the young twenty-somethings in the same job arena. You now know why are so excited about coming to work every day, while most of them are still trying to figure out how to balance a checkbook. Even if it is not a new career, but just a satisfying hobby, this activity can also be the reason you get out of bed every day during your retirement.

Don't be afraid to let your passion build. You might not even know today what it is; but you will know it when it is uncovered and it is staring you right in the face. Embrace that new-found passion and unleash its power so you can truly enjoy where it takes you. You just might end up going down roads that you never even knew were there!

5 - FINANCES are IMPORTANT, but they are not the only ingredient to a successful retirement

I would love to know how many books have been published, and how many seminars are being offered, on the financial aspects of retirement. Can you say thousands and tens of thousands? There might even be more than that. Wow, that's a lot! If that tells you nothing else, all those books and all those seminars should be telling you that you must have your "financial stuff" all together when you are ready to retire. Is that news to you? I didn't think so. Let's acknowledge right now how important it is to be financially ready for retirement. I know that; you know that, and most of the millions of future retirees know that.

That's good because that means that I don't have to talk about that in this book.

As I have said before, you should always consult with a financial advisor when you are making serious financial decisions; and retirement is one of the most serious financial decisions that you will ever make! I have to make the assumption that you are already working with a financial advisor to ensure that your retirement will be financially sound – if you're not working with one, then I urge you to start working with one to make those plans.

What do you do if you don't know a financial advisor? The first place I would go is to the local branch where you do your banking. Tell them you are looking for some help in doing your financial planning as you are planning for your retirement. Jot down some notes and say, "Thanks – let me think about this and get back with you." Go through the same process at the other places where you have financial accounts – your credit union, brokerage firm, insurance company, etc. Also talk to two or three close friends whom you feel are somewhat financially savvy. Ask them if they have a financial advisor, and how comfortable do they feel with that person. Set up an appointment and talk to their financial advisors. Once you have talked with all of them, think about which one makes you feel the most comfortable. If one of them was pushing you to set up an account right away – scratch him off the list. He just wants your money. You need to feel that your financial advisor cares more about you than he does about himself. After all, it is your future and your money – you have the right to expect that of him (or her of course).

Moving beyond the financial planning aspect of retirement (remembering that's not the focus of this book), there are other serious aspects to your retirement that you must pay attention to or else you will be setting yourself up for a less than optimal (also read as "unhappy") retirement. That is the reason for the title of this chapter telling you that your finances might be all set, but those finances are not the only thing that you need for your successful retirement.

We touched on one of those additional items in the previous chapter when we talked about the passion to do something really special in your retirement. This passion can be a new source of activities for you that give you a whole new meaning for life, and these new activities might even be a new way for you to make some money – although that's not always the prime motivator behind these new passions. Our parents and grandparents looked at retirement as the time in their lives when they could just sit back and relax and do practically nothing. The generation that is nearing retirement now wants to do more in retirement and they expect that they will be able to continue to do the things in retirement that they have enjoyed doing. The "boomer generation" is not retiring to the rocking chair on the front porch!

I personally believe that the most important ingredient to a successful retirement is a well-thought plan of the things you want to do while you are retired. I didn't underline or add other emphasis to "well-thought," but perhaps

I should have. Having a retirement plan is a good thing, but a well-thought retirement plan is worth its weight in gold. You have worked many years to get to this point in your life when you are now able to focus more on the things that you want to do rather than the things that you have to do. It would be a shame to arrive at this juncture ("retirement") without a real plan on the things that you want to do now that you have actually arrived there. The sad truth, however, is that many people do exactly that – they expect that "retirement" will show them the things to do. Sorry, folks, but retirement is a phase in your life; it is not an activity that drives your actions. You have to be in charge of your retirement, or else all you will do is sit in your rocking chair on the front porch and wave to the neighbors as they stroll by or as they are headed off on another trip. You did not buy this book to do that.

A key ingredient to your well-thought plan for retirement is what you already learned in the earlier chapter, (WHY you MUST START "retiring" 10 years in advance)." If you wait until you actually retire before you begin doing the things that you think you might want to do in retirement, you will be disappointed. This disappointment will stem from things that you could have already been enjoying but you delayed doing until you "retired." It will also stem from things you think you will enjoy – and you will have committed considerable resources toward doing – but you then find out that you don't really enjoy them. I'll cover this in more detail in a later chapter (How to AVOID some of the MISTAKES made by many retirees). This is an admittedly negative viewpoint but it is one that does exist in the way that people plan (or fail to plan) their retirement.

A more positive way to address your retirement activities is if you have a plan of what you want to do once you retire, and you start doing the things in that plan before you retire – then your retirement activities will flow as a natural extension from your pre-retirement life. This again follows naturally from the material in an earlier chapter. My wife and I felt that we would enjoy vacationing in certain areas (warm beach climates) once we retired. In preparation for our retirement and the times we could enjoy in those areas, we began purchasing timeshare properties in the locations where we knew we would want to visit when we retired. This way we would have already experienced those places, and they would be paid for by the time we retired. So as it turns out, the only financial burden that these timeshares have now that I am retired is the annual maintenance fee which is nothing compared with the price of the same amount of time in a quality hotel in that area.

The other primary ingredient to our successful retirement is that we have developed a list of the places we want to go and the things that we want do. I go into more detail on this in a later chapter (SIX DOCUMENTS that you must have). Our particular list is flexible in that we are always discussing the merits of a particular place or activity, and we even occasionally remove an item and replace it with another. The most important thing is that we are constantly evaluating our retirement activities, and even reprioritizing the things that we want to do. This part of it – adding, removing, and reprioritizing the items – is actually a very healthy part of your retirement (and possibly even a healthy part of your personal relationship). My wife and I make fun about my "flexibility" or the lack thereof. I have actually been working very hard to be more flexible about the things that we do in our own retirement. My Capricorn nature drives me to want to do everything that I want to do right way. I am working to be more flexible to say that it is okay if we don't do that particular thing this year; we can always do it next year, or the year after that.

As you read further into this book, you are going to figure out that I like to "vacation." I have always liked to travel, and I view each travel trip as a vacation, even if it is actually a business trip. Part of that is a mental attitude that you can be on vacation no matter where you are. It doesn't matter if you want your retirement to include a lot of travel and vacation, or if you are more content to "stay at home." The most important thing is that you must have a

35

plan for the things that you want to do when you are retired. That way, whether you are busy traveling all over the world or sitting at home reading the classic books you have always wanted to read – no matter what it is you are doing – you will be happy because you are living the retirement life that you have planned for yourself.

6 - How to AVOID some of the MISTAKES made by many retirees

There are going to be some people who are a little set off (or maybe even more than "a little") by what I am going to say in this chapter. You may have done some of these things, or you have friends and family who have done them. I apologize to you right now because I am calling them a mistake, which means that there is the implication that you, your friends, or your family has made these mistakes. We all have made mistakes; I know plenty of people who would gladly tell you that I have certainly made my share of them – maybe even more than my share.

The reason for this chapter is to tell you what I have observed that many retirees have done, and that I would caution you to be more prepared before you get into the same situation. As with many things in life, there is not always a single right or wrong answer to everything. You might know someone who did what I call a mistake, but that it was the best thing they could have ever done. Good for them. Remember, I am talking in generalizations here and also just from general observations. I have not performed any scientific studies; these are just from things that I have seen people do once they have gotten close to retirement, or they have done them after they retired. One last note: Even if you decide to knowingly do one of the following items, at least you will be more prepared for some of the possible results – knowledge can be a powerful tool.

Many readers make a usually accurate assumption that items near the top of a listing are more important than the items farther down the list. This is one time when that thinking is erroneous. Because I have not done any scientific studies as to the frequency of occurrence or the resulting financial impact, I would be doing you a disservice by saying that any one of these is more important – or more detrimental – to you than any of the others. Feel free to make notes of the ones that you want to be more aware of, or the ones that you have already observed in others (or even yourself).

- **Buy an RV but had never been RV'ing before** – I would love to know how many millions of dollars are spent by new retirees each year on brand new motor homes and other recreational vehicles (pull-along trailers, fifth-wheel trailers, etc.). They are fun to look at, and the appeal of being the first owner hooks many first-time purchasers. The first paragraph on the home page of a major RV dealer starts, "Nothing compares with the freedom and exhilaration of the [*name of the RV dealership*] experience. Once you're behind the wheel, the open road is your passport to destinations you could have only imagined." So how can it be a mistake if they tell you that buying an RV gets you freedom, exhilaration, and the ability to go anywhere you want? Oh, that's right – they are the ones who want to sell you that RV.

  I think that owning a recreational vehicle can be a fantastic experience that does provide all those things that the dealership says it will. But here is where I think it is a mistake. Notice that the title of this section says that it is a mistake for retirees to buy an RV when they had <u>not</u> been RV'ing before. How do they know that they are going to like this new way of travel and living when they have not previously experienced it? My wife and I have talked many times that one of the things we wanted to do when we retired was to travel in an RV around the country. The only RV that we have ever traveled "in" is a small pop-up trailer. It has been a very good trailer, and we used it extensively when our children we smaller – we visited all the National Parks in the western United States. It wasn't always the ideal situation (putting it up and talking it down during the pouring rain at Mt. Rainier was not fun). We still have that pop-up that we bought in 1990, and we continue to use it for camping.

But the key point is that I am not about to go buying a motor home or a larger trailer without having rented one to try it out first. If you think you want to have a motor home, then you must rent one to see if that style of traveling and living is something that you can enjoy for an extended period of time. Rent one for a 4-day weekend or for a week vacation. If you like it, then rent one for a longer vacation- such as two weeks or more. Just don't run out and buy one without having tried it first. You might be able to afford it, even paying cash for it. But this is a serious commitment of time, money, and work that you do not want to jump headfirst into without first sampling it. If you don't believe me – do this and then write me to tell me I am wrong. Go visit some of the larger RV dealerships in your area. Ask them if they have any RVs that are less than one year old with fewer than 10,000 miles on them. See how many they have, and then ask them what the situations were with them. Why do they have them back for sale after such a short period of time?

- **Don't have a written plan of things to do and places to go** – It could be an easy temptation to enter retirement with the motto of "I'll do whatever I want to do." After many years of hard work and dedication, the thought of not having to do anything according to a schedule has a certain appeal that is easy to want. The only problem with this philosophy is that it then becomes too easy to fall into the trap of not really doing the things that you have always said you wanted to do when you retired. That would be a shame.

There is a section in the next chapter (SIX DOCUMENTS that you must have) that addresses this mistake. I feel that it is critical to have a list of "what you want to do and where you want to go" in retirement so that you can accomplish those goals that you made many years ago. There is

39

nothing wrong with taking some time off and "doing nothing," but you would not be reading this book if that is how you wanted to spend your whole retirement. When you are making your list, don't get bogged down by practicality or current financial feasibility; if it is something you want to do or somewhere you want to go, it should be on your list. Look at your list frequently. Has something new surfaced that should be on the list? Have any priorities changed? Has your health changed so you should drop something from the list, or something should be moved up so you can do it "while you can"? Even though it is on your "wish/want list," you most likely will not accomplish all of them. That's okay; you probably still accomplished more of your retirement activities goals than people who don't have theirs written down.

- **Think their money will last forever** – This will be an extremely short section because I have told you many times that I am not a financial consultant or advisor. That is also why I list a "Financial Consultant" as one of the four people you must know well, and vice versa, in another chapter (FOUR PEOPLE you should know very well, and vice versa). Refer to that chapter, and then work with your financial consultant(s) to make sure that your financial situation meets your current and future needs.

- **Don't spend any money for fear that it won't last long enough** – This is almost the exact opposite of the previous section. These retirees heard many times from their parents (or grandparents) how tough it was during the Great Depression, and they do not want to be in that same situation. Many of these people have hundreds of thousands of dollars, even millions of dollars in assets, but they also feel that they can never have too much money. It is not like they are trying to amass large amounts of wealth to live well, travel frequently, and share with others. They still live a modest life and do very little in retirement that will do anything to draw down on their savings.

I have always felt that Americans as a whole do not save enough money. The ironic thing is that we are taxed on the earnings of our savings, yet we receive a tax break for certain expenditures. That sure sounds like a backwards incentive program to me. But I am not an economist. There is nothing wrong with savings, and there is nothing wrong with making sure that your savings do last for as long as you want them to (including passing money on to heirs and charitable organizations). Once again, here is why it is critical to work with a financial consultant (or possibly more than one) to make sure that your money will last the right amount of time for you. Refer to the section on Financial Consultant in the later chapter (FOUR PEOPLE you should know very well, and vice versa).

- **Expect to be able to do the same things with their non-retired friends** – I have seen this same phenomenon occur when couples have their first child. The friends with whom they used to do things all of a sudden become not as available to them. Why? Because their friends have no children and that used to be one of the bonds that allowed them to do things together. But that similarity changes now that the one couple has a child. The couple with the child now begins to have more in common with other couples with children. They will attend the same birthday parties; they will swap children for a date night without children; they will eventually attend the same school functions and just spend more time together. It is not that they no longer like their friends who have no children; this new addition to their life changes the dynamics of the people that they tend to gravitate to.

It is quite natural for people to want to maintain the same pattern of activities with their acquaintances. After all, these are the people we have

41

spent time with, gone to dinner with, and we might have even traveled with them. But there is a change now, and it is you (the retiree) who is the one who has changed. You now have more time to do things along with the freedom of picking <u>when</u> you want to do them. The only problem is that your non-retired friends still have their regular schedules that they must adhere to (working and other work-related obligations; limited vacation and possibly even strict vacation times, etc.). You will try to do a few things with them, but you will eventually find out that you are slowly moving apart from them. Both of you will attempt to maintain the relationship; but just as a garden requires care and cultivation or it will go to seed and be overrun with weeds, you will have to work even harder to keep that relationship the same.

Just because the relationships with your friends are going to change doesn't mean that you will never see them; just less frequently. The positive to all of this is that you will gradually develop an additional set of friends who were previously no more than mild acquaintances – other retirees. Cultivate these new relationships and you will soon find yourself learning and doing new things with them.

▪ **Expect huge changes to happen automatically** – Even though retirement is typically triggered by a specific activity (actually retiring) on a specific date (your actual retirement date), I consider "retirement" to be more of a state of mind than a statement of your working situation. And because you have heeded the advice in a previous chapter, and you have started retiring 10 years' in advance, your retirement will gradually ramp up rather than just instantaneously jumping out at you. Just as we don't notice how our own children are growing because we see them every day, their aunts and uncles are amazed when they haven't seen them for a year or two. "My, how you have grown," is a typical reaction.

This is also how your retirement happens. Because you are working on it for five to ten years, it just gradually happens. Thus, you are not going to see or feel any revolutionary changes, and this is actually a very good thing. The people who do see significant changes in their lives are the ones who have not started retiring as you are going to do. They retire on a Friday afternoon, and they get up on Monday morning and find out that their entire world changed over the weekend. This is not healthy for the new retiree or for the family. Studies have shown that these retirees have a significantly shorter life span after retirement than those who phase into retirement and the changes that come along with retirement.

- **Say, "Now we will start traveling," even though they had not done much traveling before** – I think you know that I love to travel. If you didn't already know that, now you do. My enjoyment of travel may have been initiated by being raised in a military family where we moved every two years up until I was in junior high school. My dad retired from the Navy, and so that was the end of the moving as part of our family. I traveled all over the world while I was working, and my wife and our family have also enjoyed travel as part of our vacations in the US, to Europe, the Caribbean, and to Mexico. So travel is not new to us, and it is something that we will continue to do in our retirement.

My wife and I know people who have not traveled a whole lot – a big trip for them might be to the neighboring state. Don't take me wrong, there is nothing inherently wrong with not wanting to vacation in Mexico, in Aruba, or in Paris, France. What I do call "wrong" is when these people retire and then say they are going to go to those places and do the things that we have done after going back to the same place several times. Why do I say that? Because these people have not traveled much before, they really don't know that they are going to like it, and they may be very disappointed if it doesn't meet their expectations. Just like the retirees in

43

the first section in this chapter who buy the RV when they retire, these new retiree travelers do not have the experience to know "how" to travel. They might not even have a passport, meaning that international travel will be delayed until they get one. Whether it is the lack of a passport or something else that disappoints them, they will soon realize that travel is not the panacea that they thought it was going to be. That is a real shame because travel can be a very rewarding and educational experience. But it is like cooking, gardening, or even reading – you just cannot start doing it one day and enjoy it immediately. It takes practice, and you should get your practice long before you retire if you want to be able to take full advantage of all the benefits of travel. See the longest chapter in this book (VACATION SECRETS from a seasoned traveler) for some helpful hints.

- **Travel "on the cheap"** – I love to save money just as much as the next person does. One of the travel mistakes that I have seen – I have even done it myself, but I am getting "better" – is to try to spend as little money as possible while on vacation. Again, there is nothing wrong with saving money, but a key part of travel is to enjoy the local settings, the food, and the activities that are special to that area. And you cannot do those things by just sitting in your room and reading a book that you brought with you. (My wife will shoot me for saying that because she <u>loves</u> to read, and she always has many books with her; no matter where we go.)

There are ways you can travel well without spending your life savings, and I give you some of those hints and tips in a later chapter. While it is not essential to spend a lot of money to have a good time when you travel, you don't want to return home disappointed because you were afraid to spend money for a once-in-a-lifetime experience (such as a helicopter ride into the volcanoes in Hawaii). You have to be the judge and set your own budget when you travel. All I recommend is that you do spend enough money so you can honestly say to yourself that you really did enjoy where you went and what you did.

- **Switch to conservative investments immediately**– I am not going to spend too much time here, because this is one of the numerous reasons why you must work with an experienced financial consultant – see the chapter (FOUR PEOPLE you should know well, and vice versa). All I will say is that I have seen retirees change their entire investment strategy when they retired because they were taught by their parents that they should only have "conservative" investments in retirement. There is certainly nothing wrong with Certificates of Deposit or other "risk-avoidance" investments, but your financial consultant will explain to you why these have their own forms of risk.

- **Think they have to do only "old folks' activities"** – I am a "card carrying" member of AARP, and I joined just as soon as I turned 50. But belonging to AARP does not mean that I am only going to do things that "retired people" do. Personally, I don't see that there is any distinction between what a person does before retirement versus after retirement. Just because you are entering retirement doesn't mean that you are entering a retirement home. I have seen people in their 70s surfing some pretty good waves. There was even a very well-known gentleman in Idaho who was still snow skiing at age 85 – and he was not just going down the bunny slopes either.

These people might be exceptions, but I wouldn't say that they are exceptional, either. They were just continuing to do the activities that they had done for many, many years. They were not going to let "retirement" slow them down and keep them from doing the things that they truly enjoyed. If you have never surfed, it is highly unlikely that you are going to take it up on your next trip to Hawaii. And I don't expect that you will get your SCUBA certification just because you are planning to visit the Great Barrier Reef on your 4-week trip to Australia.

The key is to enjoy life when you are retired – and that usually means to enjoy doing the things that have already brought you enjoyment in your life. I like to play shuffleboard; it is a lot of fun on a cruise ship when you have to figure out if the puck is going to curve left or right depending on the rolling of the ship. But I am not going to take up shuffleboard just because I am retiring and I think that is what retired people do. Some people have said that you are only as old as you think you are. If you subscribe to that theory – and it is a good one to believe in – do the things that you want to do because you enjoy doing them. Maybe you are the oldest one in the badminton tournament or in the sandcastle building contest – who cares? If you are doing something that you enjoy, do like that famous commercial says, and "Just do it."

- **Want to use the benefits from insurance policies because "I paid for it"** – This was one of my Mom's pet peeves. She turned 90 and we celebrated it with a great birthday party at the Hard Rock Café in Las Vegas, NV. We chose going to Las Vegas because it was a "neutral site" and it allowed many people to attend rather than if we had held it where one of the sons lived (I am in Idaho, and my brothers were in California). We held the party at the Hard Rock Café because she had a blast at the Hard Rock Café in Copenhagen, Denmark, when we were on a cruise there a few years' earlier.

For a while, about once a week she would bring up the fact that she had been paying for years for her Long Term Care insurance. "Maybe I will just move into a home and let the insurance pay for it," is how the discussion typically would begin. Her thinking was that she deserved to receive the benefits because she had been paying the premiums. So we had to go through the process again that she must meet certain requirements in

46

order to receive the benefits – such as inability to feed herself, dress herself, etc. Even though she was 90 and lived alone in her condominium unit, she was able to take care of herself. Thus, she did not qualify to receive those benefits.

She and others in her situation have two choices – continue to pay the premiums for when you <u>will</u> <u>need</u> <u>the</u> <u>assistance,</u> or stop paying for the insurance policy. I am not going to make any recommendations at all on that decision. That is something that you would want to discuss with your family and possibly with your attorney and other trusted advisors. So whether it is your long term care policy or insurance that provides some other coverage, don't feel that the insurance company "owes you" something, and that you must get it. Even if you have not already received any benefits from an insurance policy, you have received something from it – peace of mind that you do have benefits in case you have to use it. It's the same as the insurance you have on your house or your car(s). Do you really want a house fire or a car collision so you can collect on the insurance? I didn't think so.

- **Don't question doctors who keep adding prescriptions to their list of medicines without removing any** – I consider myself to be extremely fortunate in that I am not taking any medications on a regular basis. Sure, I take a pain reliever occasionally for the aches and pains that come along, but I have no prescriptions that I take daily, weekly, or monthly. I would say it is because "I have lived a clean life," but then my wife corrects me – I am just lucky <u>so</u> <u>far</u>.

The pharmaceutical companies provide a wonderful service by researching and developing drugs that can help us in so many ways, and I applaud them for that. I do have a concern, however, when a doctor prescribes a medicine for someone and possibly has not even asked to review the list of medications that the person is already taking. I am not an

MD, and I have not taken any pharmacy courses. But it is hard for me to believe that there is not some interaction that occurs when a person is taking many prescriptions.

Maybe your doctor <u>does</u> <u>know</u> every medication you are taking, and he or she is able to determine that there is no problem in your continuing to take each one of them. I am sure that some doctors do, and they are doing you a huge favor when they do. But you owe it to yourself and to your family to ask your doctor, "Do I need to keep taking every one of these medications? Do you know if there is any interaction between them?" Listen to your doctor's answer, or even the tone of his or her voice. Remember, it is your body and your life – make sure you are comfortable with the answer you are hearing. If you are not comfortable with the answer you are hearing from your doctor, I recommend that you consult with your family and your other trusted advisors to consider using the services of another doctor. Sorry, doctors, but your patients deserve the very best that you (or perhaps another doctor) have to offer.

- **Make drastic changes to their lifestyle** – Similar to the retirees mentioned above who switch to all conservative investments, these retirees start doing different things and doing things completely differently because they are now "retired." Oh what a mistake!

    I don't know how many times I have already said it, but I am going to say it again. You don't have to change the things you do – your lifestyle – just because you are entering the retirement phase of your life. Sure, you might do some things a *little differently* – you might stop going down the double black diamond ski slopes, but you are not going to give up skiing completely. Your adventure vacations might begin to change from vigorous hiking to easier trails, but you are not going to stop going on vacations where you can walk and see the natural sights.

Enjoy your retirement; just don't make such major changes that might even get you to start thinking if you made a mistake by retiring. That is never a mistake. Remember, retirement is an essential phase of your life – ENJOY RETIREMENT AND ENJOY LIFE!

7 - SIX DOCUMENTS that you must have

You might already have most, if not all, of the six documents that I list in this chapter as being extremely important to you and to your retirement life. If you do already have them (or even half of them), let me say, "Good job." You have shown that you are already planning well for yourself and your family in your retirement transition. This is just my list; other might say you need to have many more medical documents, for example. I have no argument with them if they want to add more to my list. Perhaps you, too, can add more once you have the basic six. After reading this chapter and the rest of the book, you might even decide that there is one of these six documents that you feel that you do <u>not</u> need. That is okay; at least I have done my job of informing you of the main documents that most people entering retirement should have, and keep updated.

Please remember that I am not an attorney, and therefore I am not rendering any legal advice to you. **<u>You should always work with a competent advisor with whom you are very comfortable when you are dealing in legal matters such as wills and powers of attorney</u>**. The information I am providing, however, is deemed to be reliable and is from public sources.

<u>Will</u> – You already have a will, and so does everyone. Did you know that? It might not be the will that accomplishes what you want accomplished, but everyone has a will even if they have not filled one out and personally signed it. You must be asking, "Then how do they have a will?" The answer is that each state provides for the disposition of a person's property through the process of probate. Again, the court's method of disposition and distribution of your property is most likely not how you want it to be handled; but that is the way it is.

Because you want to have control over how your property is distributed, you need to have a will (Usually called a "Last Will and Testament") created for you by a competent legal advisor. I know I have used the word *competent* many times, and that is not to imply that I think there are *in*competent advisors. The meaning of competent in this situation is that you want a legal advisor who is knowledgeable in the particular area, and who is licensed to practice law in your state. Your brother-in-law might handle divorce cases in another state, but that does not make him competent and qualified to draft your will. He might be able to get you started, but you still want a <u>competent legal advisor</u> in your state to review it and to complete it.

You can buy a blank form in most office supply stores, and there are plenty of free forms available online. Use one of them as a starting point so that you have an idea of the matters that you need to address in your will. But then take it to a qualified person to complete it, pay the bill, and then rest assured that you have done the right and legal thing to protect your interests – not only today but also once you have passed away.

There is a specialty in the legal profession that is not that well known; it is "elder care." There are attorneys who have chosen to specialize in this field, and some of them are able to go by the designation of "Certified Elder Law Attorney." There is a link to the National Elder Law Foundation in the Reference Materials chapter, so you can find out more about Elder Law attorneys, what their focus is, and where you can find one. Given the serious nature of the legal affairs as one gets older (or as one's parent gets older), these CELA's provide a most valuable service. I highly recommend that you seek one in your area as you update your will and other important legal documents. Once you are comfortable with that person, make sure that your parent's wills, etc., are current and provide the proper instructions.

Living Will – A living will is essentially a statement that you do not want to be kept alive by "artificial means." These documents vary from state to state because of the different laws that are in effect. Excerpted language from a Living Will for California might read, "If I should have an incurable and irreversible condition that has been diagnosed by two physicians and that will result in my death within a relatively short time without the administration of life-sustaining treatment or has produced an irreversible coma or persistent vegetative state, and I am no longer able to make decisions regarding my medical treatment, I direct my attending physician, pursuant to the Natural Death Act of California, to withhold or withdraw treatment, including artificially administered nutrition and hydration, that only prolongs the process of dying or the irreversible coma or persistent vegetative state and is not necessary for my comfort or to alleviate pain." [http://www.freelegalforms.net/index.cfm?index=forms&filename=Form1258 0.htm]

Unlike the Will in the section above, the Living Will also has certain moral and religious aspects to it. It is not for everyone, and so you should really make sure that the wording and the actions are the ones that you want. Of course, you want to make sure this is written and reviewed by your competent legal advisor so that it will hold up in court should it be challenged in the case of your incapacitation or other condition that you have devised your living will to cover. Don't keep this hidden away as if it were some secret. Make sure that your primary care physician and your attorney each have a copy of it. If you move into any community facility (a retirement home, an assisted living facility, etc.), they will generally require that you have one of these on file.

Durable Power of Attorney – A power of attorney is a legal form that is typically drafted to cover a single specific activity or transaction. For example, a husband might sign a power of attorney for the sale of their house, and give it to his wife before he leaves on an extended business trip. That way, she could handle all the affairs of the selling of the house while he is gone.

Otherwise, there might be papers requiring his signature that would have to wait until his return to be completed – this might hinder the completion of the sale. A Durable Power of Attorney is typically an all-encompassing power of attorney form in which one person (your mother, perhaps) signs over the power for you to make any decisions <u>and</u> actions regarding any of her activities, properties, etc. You want to have a durable power of attorney naming your most trusted person (typically your spouse or significant other; although in rare cases it might be someone else) as your "lawful attorney with full power . . ." Because of the significant impact that this person can have over your affairs, you should review your intentions with this person and then have both of you meet with your legal advisor to develop your Durable Power of Attorney <u>exactly</u> as you want it to operate.

Passport – Most people who already do some or a lot of travel already have their passport; it's an absolute requirement if you cross any US border. You can ignore this one if you live in a region where you do not need a passport to travel between countries. But since most of my readers live in the US, I want to stress the importance of having a US Passport. First of all, it is the most widely accepted form of identification ANYWHERE in the world. Yes, maybe the local convenience store clerks would prefer to see your Driver's License, but maybe that is why they're working in the convenience store. You might be saying, "I don't need a passport because I am not planning any overseas vacations." And you might not be – right now at least. I had an acquaintance who had the opportunity to take a trip to Europe, but he had to decline because he did not have a passport.

One of the story morals in my book *Parables for Life in the 21st Century* is, "Is it better to have it and not need it, or need it and not have it?" With the tighter requirements placed on travel to Canada and to Mexico from the US, the time it takes to get a new passport, or even a renewal, has increased tremendously. I strongly recommend that you apply for yours right away. It is valid for 10 years, and having one will eliminate a major reason (or excuse) for not taking that trip to Europe, or even flying down to one of the Caribbean islands. For those of you whose passports are expiring in the next year, I suggest that you go ahead and apply for a renewal as soon as you know when you will have a two-month window of not traveling outside the US. Don't wait until it is too late! See the Reference Materials chapter for additional passport information.

Comprehensive listing of Assets – Most people have a rough idea of what their assets are, especially as they are getting closer to retirement. This is because they want to make sure that they "have enough" to be able to retire. But that is not the only reason for having this list, a very comprehensive list of all of your assets. Even though I have called this a list of your assets, you also need to include your debts so you have a true picture of your financial situation. While I do not know very many people who want to fully disclose to their family members everything that they have, they would want them to know about it in case of death or an incapacitating illness. You might, for example, own property in another state, and there is no legal recording of that property in your own state. A search of the county records or the state records in your home state would not reveal the existence of this property and so your heirs would have no knowledge of it. Include with this listing any appraisals or other information that you might have for jewelry, artwork and other collectibles.

In essence, you are assembling a small notebook that will expedite the process should you need the information or when you die. The format of how you compile this information is not critical – the key is to just have it. Once you have all this information in one place, review it on a regular basis to ensure that it stays accurate and current. I am not talking about updating stock prices daily; I am referring to a monthly or quarterly review with your spouse or significant other to ensure that you are not leaving something off the list by mistake. During one of these regular reviews you might even decide that you really don't need that piece of art or that raw land in another state, and that you would rather sell it and take a cruise, or go on a guided tour of Italy. It is easy to forget about many items unless you are reviewing this list on a regular basis – "out of sight, out of mind" is applicable here.

List of "what you want to do and where you want to go" during retirement – If you don't know where you want to go when you are retired, it's highly unlikely that you will go there. I know that sounds silly, but the point is that you have to think about the places you want to go and the things that you want to do, and then plan when you will go there or when you will do them. We all have dream vacations – mine is a 3- to 6-month round-the-world cruise. I don't know if I will ever take it, but it is always fun to think about. Not just the cruise itself, but being able to take the time to totally relax and not worry about anything else for that period of time. You can put your dream vacation on this list, but it is more important to put all the other little things that you have always talked about. Maybe it is camping in Bryce Canyon National Park and waking up early to see the sunrise over the beautiful red cliffs. Maybe it is volunteering at the food bank, with Meals on Wheels, or at a senior center. Are there some states that you have always wanted to visit? Add those to the list. Once you have some items on your list – I have included my list format in the Reference Materials chapter – you can then fill in the rest of the information, such as your priority, when you want to do it, maybe even how much you think it will cost, etc. Modify my template so it works for you. You should keep the items on the list even after you have completed them. That way you can look back at see what you have actually done in your retirement.

8 - VACATION SECRETS from a seasoned traveler

I consider every day a "vacation day" now that I am retired. Of course, many of those vacation days are spent at home, and I am going to guess that you really don't care much about those days or what I do when I go on a true vacation. What you do care about and what you want out of this chapter are the following:

- How you can get some good deals when you travel

- Why "vacation specials" might not be that special

- Some of the untold secrets of airline travel

- How I have "gotten the most" out of my travels, and how you can also

- Good, bad, and ugly views of timeshare properties

- Steps to planning your "ideal vacation"

You are probably wondering how I am qualified to tell you all these things because no where have I said anything about being in the travel industry. You are right; I have never been employed in the travel industry. What I have done is a LOT of travel; so much, in fact, that I had to have additional pages added to my passport because all the original pages had been filled with immigration stamps from countries all over the world. I have traveled for work; I have traveled for pleasure; sometimes I was even able to combine work and pleasure. When I was still working for my last company, there were times that our travel organization would actually call me to ask for my advice on certain overseas travel – what were the best routes to take; what hotels would I recommend to be close to "the office"; which seats are better than others on long flights; how should they get from the airport to the hotel, etc.? Because of my knowledge and all my travels, I now have the U.S. Registered Trademark

America's International Travel Expert®, and I'm the only person in the world who can have that trademark!

Now that I am spending a lot of time writing, I am able to travel to specific locations for writing, which means I am able to be where I want to be while I write (which means I accomplish both "work" and pleasure), and I get to receive certain tax benefits. I know there a lot of people who do not want to do much traveling, especially after they have retired from a life of traveling for work, so this chapter will probably not hold much interest for them. But for the majority of retirees who do want to "hit the road" and travel, get ready to take notes. You are now about to be given access to a lot of vacation secrets that I have gathered over the years, but ones that I have never given to anyone else. While these are "my secrets," I expect you to use them to your own benefit. I cannot stop you if you want to share them with others – just remember that the more people who know about them, the less valuable they might become for you.

How you can get some good deals when you travel

A good deal is only a "good deal" if it is something that you want to do, when you are able to do it, and if the stated value actually is of value to you. Spending a week in Aspen, Colorado in the middle of ski season does not appeal to everyone. If you don't like to ski, or even if you just don't want to spend a vacation in a cold climate, then being offered a fantastic deal in Aspen will not register as a "good deal" for you. Even if it were free, you still might not have any interest. So keep that in mind – a good deal has to be a good deal for you. I'm going to repeat that again – with some added emphasis this time – so that is becomes a part of your everyday thinking: "A good deal <u>has</u> to be a <u>good</u> <u>deal</u> for *you!*"

The most important word to remember when you are looking for a good travel deal is "flexibility." If you are flexible in terms of when you can travel (not only <u>when</u> during the year, but also how soon can you leave?), you will generally be able to find better deals available to you. Once again, **flexibility** can be your friend in travel. You might say, "Sure, once you're retired you can be flexible. But I'm not retired; so how does that help me?"

It works the same whether you are retired or not. Here is how it works. You pick a weekend, a week, two weeks, a month – whatever period of time you want to go on vacation. Mark that time on your calendar, and schedule it as "vacation." If you still work, then make sure everyone knows you will be gone then. Don't fret that you have scheduled your time off but that you don't know where you are going. At least not yet.

In the chapter on Reference Materials, I list some websites that advertise that they have last-minute travel deals. Take a look at them and try this exercise. When you go to their site, see what "deals" they have if you wanted to leave on the next day, or a couple days later, or maybe even next week. Do they have enough of a variety of the places and activities where you would consider going, if it were the right price? How do the prices seem to you? You can also go visit a local travel agency and tell them what you would like to do – tell them when you want to travel and that you are willing to be flexible in terms of location if it's a "good deal." See if the travel agent is willing to work with you and provide you with the information that you want. If you don't feel comfortable with that travel agent, go to another one. The airlines sometimes have last-minute deals, but you have to either keep checking their websites or sign up for the "last-minute deals" emails from them.

That's taken care of, so now let's go ahead and find some travel deals that you <u>do</u> consider to be good deals for you. Most people have particular places where they would like to go (or have gone to before and would consider going back). If that fits you, then write down the places where you would like to go.

This is your list, so you don't have to be practical about these places. If you have never been to Paris, France, and you want to go there – write it on your list. If you want to visit Sydney, Australia, or go on a photographic safari in Africa – write it down. Maybe it is a historical site around Virginia or Washington, DC. Perhaps it is a state park or a national park that you have read about (or seen on the Travel Channel). It doesn't matter where it is – if it is someplace where you want to go – then it needs to be on your list. You will be coming back to this list a little bit later, so don't feel that you have to list all of the locations the very first time.

Now that your vacation places are written down, go back and note if there are particular times or events in the year that would make the trip more enjoyable. For example, perhaps you like to watch and play tennis, and you have said you would like to go see the Australian Open sometime. Why not combine that event (in late January of each year) with that trip you want to take to Sydney? It looks like a late January-early February trip would be the best time for that one. Or sticking with the tennis theme, the French Open is in Paris in June – so that is when you would want to schedule that trip. Of course the opposite can also be true. Perhaps you do not want to be in one of your vacation spots when there is a special event. Writing down these times will also help you as you are considering all possibilities. A popular trip is the "Fall Colors" throughout the Northeast in October. You could combine a historical trip through Boston while you are working your way up the coast to Maine.

TIP: I have provided a template for this vacation list-making in the Reference Materials – feel free to make copies of it and then use it as you think about the places you want to go.

Once you have your wish list made, contact a professional travel agent either at a full-service agency or at your local Auto Club office. Take your list with you and let the travel agent know your priorities and your flexibility. Ask him or her to contact you only if a "really good deal" pops up. Saving 30% on travel is commonplace; you want to save a minimum of 50% - preferably 60% - 75%. Why not; it's your money!

Another way to find a good deal on the places where you want to go is to subscribe to a service that notifies you of last-minute deals. Remember I said that you needed to be flexible. I list some websites in the Reference Materials that I found by typing "last-minute deals" into an online search engine. I have not used any of these services, so I cannot attest to the level of service or value you might receive from them. But there are a lot of these websites, so if you don't find what you want at the first one, go to the next one.

An old-fashioned way to get a good deal when you travel, but I have had it work for me, is to simply ask for something. My wife and I were going to Aruba for a week in the summer of 2000. Our two children (ages 17 and 19 at the time) were also going, and so I had booked two rooms at the Hyatt Regency there. As a frequent traveler, I had "top status" in Hyatt's Gold Passport program, and I was using points and a couple free coupons for the fourteen room nights (two rooms time seven nights). I called Hyatt Gold Passport to make sure that our rooms would be on the "Gold Passport" floor – the concierge level is another description of it. They transferred me to the Reservations Manager at the Hyatt Regency in Aruba who quickly confirmed, "Yes, Mr. Gustafson. You will be on the Gold Passport floor." Now that he said "Yes" once (am I starting to sound like a salesman now?), I continued. "I see that you have a VIP Suite; we have stayed in the VIP Suite at the Hyatt in La Jolla, CA (a true statement). Is that suite available?"

Was there any harm in my asking to stay in that suite? No harm at all. And what was the worst he could tell me. He could have said, "No," but he came back on in a minute and said, "Yes, sir. That suite will be yours for the week." Remember, we are not paying anything for the two rooms we had already reserved, and now we are put into the VIP Suite, room 927. This four-room suite normally rented for $3,000 a night (no telling how much it is now), and we had it for free. Why? Because I asked for it (the elite status helped, but they still could have said "No."). Our children thought that was really something, and, of course, we were treated like royalty while there. One day as we were strolling on the property, we stopped in a restaurant that we had not been to, and I asked if we could make reservations for dinner that night. The person at the desk looked at their reservations book as she asked for my room number. As soon as I said "927," the response was, "Of course, we'll have a nice table for the four of you." When we arrived for dinner later that evening, we had the best table in the place with a gorgeous oceanfront view and waiters at our beck and call. I asked for something special and the Hyatt gave it to me. Try it the next time you know you are going to travel.

Something I <u>always</u> do when I check into a hotel or resort is to ask if there are any better rooms or upgrades they could give me, or if there are better rates for the room I have. Sometimes, there is no change, but I have gotten better room rates as well as upgraded rooms. <u>If you don't ask, you will never get it</u>. The same thing holds for airlines, although they have been much harder to get any deals from lately (not hard to understand given how many have been in, or are still in, bankruptcy). But again, they will not offer you that better seat (Exit row with more leg room, for example) if you do not ask for it. Someone will be sitting there; it might as well be you (or me!).

Why "vacation specials" might <u>not</u> be that special

Do you take the Sunday newspaper? Have you looked in the Travel section lately and seen ads that scream "Fantastic Savings," "Special Travel Values," etc.? That seems to be standard any more. The rates being offered (typically including airfare and lodging for specific dates) might be good rates if you had your choice of when you traveled. These deals are being offered for one of two reasons: 1. Surplus inventory because there are not enough people buying the tickets at normal rates; 2. Surplus inventory because people are not traveling there at that specific time.

We like to vacation in Mexico, specifically in Baja California Sur. Our preferred time to go there is in February when it is still winter in Idaho, but it is about 70-75 in Cabo San Lucas. You won't find too many deals for that time of the year to go to Cabo. Why not? People are willing to pay the normal fares to go there because that is the desirable time. What about July and August? Well, we did that once; emphasis on once! The temperature ranges from mid 90s to low 100s, and the humidity is 80% or higher. That combination of temperature and humidity makes for a terrible time outside unless you want to spend all of your time in the swimming pool or in the air-conditioned room. Guess what? You can find a good deal to Cabo in July and August because there are not a lot of other people going then (unless they were not aware of the heat and humidity as we weren't on our first time down there). Thus, just because the travel bureau offers you a "special deal," make sure it is a deal that you want – not just that they want to unload it.

The best way to make sure the deal is a good deal – and this holds true for almost any financial transaction – is to be an aware consumer. Know where it is that you want to go, and then start researching that destination. Visit some websites as well as talk to people who have gone there, and learn all you can about the area, the activities that are available there, and if there are special events going on that might have an impact – such as an annual sporting event or fashion show or something else that could draw an enormous amount of visitors to that area. One of those events might be the reason you want to go there; but if not, then you will want to avoid it at that time. Hotels will be full and charging top rates; taxis will be unavailable, and restaurants will have no available reservations. Once again, the phrase *caveat emptor* (buyer beware) holds true – know what you are getting, and make sure it is what you want. The deals are available, but you have to search them out. If it's a deal that "anyone" can get, can it really be that good of a deal? Remember, it is your time and your money – you certainly have the right to get all you can for yourself (and your traveling companions).

Some of the untold secrets of airline travel

This will probably not come as a surprise to you, but airline travel can be quite a horrendous experience. OKAY – stop laughing! On the other hand, when things go your way, airline travel can actually be a pleasurable experience. I have experienced both ends of this spectrum. Sitting in a middle seat near the back of a packed airplane flight is not fun. Enjoying a wider seat in a quiet first class section makes that same flight much more enjoyable.

I have flown a lot over the years, anywhere from short 500-mile trips once a week to literally an around-the-world trip. That trip took me from Boise to Denver to Washington, DC to Amsterdam to Stockholm to Düsseldorf to Singapore to Sydney to Taipei to Tokyo to San Francisco to Boise. That was quite a 3-week jaunt. But one of the advantages of the extensive travel I did was earning elite status on one airline, allowing me to upgrade into first class on short, as well as long, flights. Not everyone is able to get into first class that way, so let me pass on some ideas to you that can make your airline travels more enjoyable.

One of the things that I have done several times is to book my reservation on a flight when there is at least one later flight going to the same destination. When I check in at the first airport (and you might be making a layover on your trip), I ask each person I encounter (ticket counter, gate agent, etc.) if the flight is oversold and if they "need a volunteer" to give up a seat. If the flight is wide open, they will smile and say, "No thank you." If it is close, they might ask you to sit in the departure area and wait until they do the boarding to see if they do need your seat on that flight. There are times, of course, when they are definitely oversold and they might actually be making an announcement for volunteers. In that case, walk up to the counter, and tell them that you will give up your seat and take a later flight. What will you get for your troubles? I have typically been booked on the next flight, given a confirmed seat in first class, and I have also received a travel voucher good for a free round-trip flight anywhere in the continental US valid for one year. One time I was then able to volunteer again for that second flight and take an even later flight. I arrived about six hours later than originally planned, but that was fine. As compensation for my time, I flew in first class and I was given ticket vouchers good for two round-trip flights. First class AND free flights – not a bad deal. Try that secret the next time you fly!

One secret that the airlines will not tell you is that there are some seats that are better than others – not counting first (or business) class, of course. Setting aside the first class and the business seats, let's see how you can get the best possible seats in economy class (I have also flown a lot in Economy). The most obvious way to get a "better" seat is to know what the seating configurations are on each plane for each airline that you fly. As a 1K traveler on United Airlines (that means I have flown 100,000 miles per year), I received as part of my annual elite status package a booklet that shows me the actual seating configuration in each of their planes. Whenever I was booking a flight on United I would look at the type of aircraft (Boeing 737, 757, Airbus 319, etc.), and then look for what seemed to be the "best available" seat on that flight. I was booking our travel to Europe for a four-week trip, and I specifically got flights that were on a Boeing 777. Not only were these very smooth flights, the configuration of the seats in Economy were 2-5-2. This meant 2 seats between each aisle and window, and 5 seats in the center section. Of course my wife and I wanted to sit in the 2-seat grouping. Well, I also know (from a previous flight where I write a note in my booklet) that seats 21H and 21J had much more legroom than the other seats on that side of the plane. So when I booked the flights, I asked for 21H and J and got those seats. That's nice!

I know that not everyone has access to this seating chart that United sends out to its most loyal customers. So another way is to call the airline after you make your reservation. Tell the agent on the phone that this is an extremely important trip for you, and that you need to be able to relax and arrive there as much refreshed as possible. Therefore, is there any way that they can find the best available seat for you? The worst they can say is "No," so you have nothing to lose by asking.

Does this sound too complicated? Would you like a much easier way to find the best seat on any aircraft on <u>any</u> airline? Okay, I will tell you. I have listed a website in the Reference Materials chapter that calls itself, "The ultimate source for airplane seating, in-flight amenities and airline information." I have used this "Seat Guru" site many times, and I recommend that you bookmark this site. It could become one of your "Favorites" when you plan your air travel.

The final secret that I will pass along to you for airline travel (hey, I can't tell you <u>all</u> of my secrets!) is to check for all of the possible routes to get you where you want to go. For example, let's say that you are traveling from San Francisco, California (SFO) to Atlanta, Georgia (ATL). You have many choices of airlines and routes to get you there. Once you factor in how far in advance you can book your flight (or how soon it is), you might find that you have many choices from which to choose. I recently checked fares online for this route with a 14-day advance purchase. United Airlines had a non-refundable roundtrip ticket with one-stop for $409; the nonstop ticket cost. If you wanted a refundable ticket, the one-stop ticket was $1,779, and the nonstop was $1,788. Delta Airlines had a non-refundable roundtrip ticket with one-stop for $404; but the nonstop ticket cost only $338. If you wanted the refundable ticket, the one-stop ticket was $1,228, and the nonstop was $1,116.

That's a comparison of only two airlines, but you can see that there is a significant difference between them – for the same route on the same days of travel. And it might not be a fair comparison because Atlanta is the major hub for Delta – but the point of the exercise was to show that it definitely pays (and you are the one who gets paid!) to check with different airlines, and to be realistic about really needing a refundable ticket. I never buy a refundable ticket. It's cheaper to buy travel insurance if you are that concerned.

How I have "gotten the most" out of my travels, and how you can also

I have already told you that I have traveled a lot- both in the US and all over the world. If you want to be able to get the most out of your travels – even if it is only once or twice a year – I suggest you do what I have been doing since 1994. The best thing you can do for yourself is to join the frequent traveler programs and avail yourself of all the bonuses and benefits that they have. Let me explain this to you.

Every airline that I know of has a frequent flyer program. Why do they have it, and why would they give away free flights? You don't need to think too hard about this to realize that they are "buying" your loyalty and your business. But before you feel that you are being taken advantage of, you have to look at the benefits that you [can] receive. I have done most of my airline travel on a single airline since 1994, and I have flown over 1.3 million actual paid flight miles on that airline (as of November 2014). So it is no wonder that I have received many good deals from them, including upgrades, free trips, priority seating, etc. Why not? Look how much business they have gotten directly or indirectly from me.

Do you always want to fly on only one airline? No! The airline I was referring to above is United Airlines, and I do try to fly on United when I can. But there are times when it does not make sense (time-wise or cost-wise) to use them. One recent example when I did not fly on United was flying down to Los Cabos, Mexico. To fly down to Los Cabos from Boise on United when I wanted to go there would have required me to spend an evening in either Denver or San Francisco. If it had been the end of the year and I needed that one flight to push me to a higher status level – I just might have done it. In this case I chose to fly a different airline. But, I did not pick just any airline; I chose one where I could still earn miles in my United account – meaning that I flew on a "partner airline." I did not earn any lifetime miles for that flight, but the flight miles did go into my United Mileage Plus account (Mileage Plus is the name of United Airline's frequent flyer program) where I can redeem them for free flights as well as various merchandise items. **I am not suggesting that you fly only on United Airlines**. What I am suggesting is that you join the frequent flyer programs of every airline that you think you will fly (it doesn't cost anything to join them). Then, before you go on your next flight, think about which airline it makes sense to travel on, and start earning your miles on that airline. I have listed some of the major airlines and their frequent flyer programs in the Reference Materials chapter. There is also a listing of some of the major "airline partner" programs so you can see which airlines you can fly on and still earn miles in your own airline's frequent flyer program.

Mileage update: It used to be that you had 3 years in which to use your accumulated miles, meaning that those miles would disappear if you did not have any more activity that added miles to, or subtracted miles from, your account in that 3-year period. Well, guess what! The airlines have now cut that back to 18 months. That means that if you don't fly with them within 18 months, all the miles that you had accumulated for awards are gone. So if you have miles in any frequent flyer account, check them online (or call the airline) find out when they will expire. Here's a little known secret so you can keep your miles: If you have a significant number of miles in your account but they will expire soon, you might be able to keep them by purchasing 1,000 miles from the program. Check it out – I have done it. It cost me a little money but I kept all the miles in that account (not mine, a relative's) so they could be used later. You might have to hunt around on the website, or call the program customer service, but it can be worth doing.

Flying on United is not the only way that I earn miles that I can redeem for free flights, etc. I also use the Mileage Plus Visa credit card, which is currently managed by Chase Bank. My United Mileage Plus number is on the credit card, and I earn one mile for every dollar I charge to that card, plus I earn double miles when I purchase my United Airlines tickets using the card. So I am earning miles every month even if I do not fly. Financial advisor and best-selling author Stephen Pollan will disagree with me here. In his great book *Die Broke*, he says to get rid of everyone of your credit cards. Sorry, Stephen – I will choose to disagree with you here. He has some good ideas, but he says you should not have any credit cards. I agree that we should not be "living" off them, but I find no harm in using them and paying them off each month. I do not like paying interest charges, so I do not want to have a balance carry from one month to the next. So I will continue to use my United Airlines credit card to charge my monthly purchases and earn more reward miles.

TIP: Instead of applying for an airline's credit card on line, call the toll-free number that is given and ask for the best deal you can get. Most of the credit card companies will give you a lot of bonus miles after your first purchase as well as a free companion airline voucher and maybe even an upgrade or two. The key is that you have to ask them for these bonuses.

Most major hotel chains offer the same type of loyalty programs as the airlines offer. I have listed a few of the major hotel chains in the Reference Materials chapter. You can typically find a link from their main website to their rewards program or whatever they call it. The interesting thing with these hotel programs is that most of them give you the opportunity to earn either "hotel points" or airline miles. So here is where you want to put some extra thought into your decision (although you can change your designation at any time). The simple question to ask yourself is, "When I travel, do I want to earn both airline miles and hotel points, or would I prefer them to be combined just for airline miles?" There is no simple answer here; you have to determine if you think you will traveling enough to earn a free trip or two on your airline without the hotel points being counted as airline miles? If you decide you would prefer to have the hotel points counted as airline miles, you will certainly earn that free airline ticket quicker, but you are not earning a free hotel stay. If you are finding this to be a hard decision, then have the hotel points count as airline miles. You are more likely to be staying at many different hotels than you are to be using many different airlines.

You read earlier how I had used points and bonuses to get a $3,000 per night 4-room VIP suite at the Hyatt Resort & Casino in Aruba. My loyalty in staying mostly in Hyatt hotels was rewarded quite handsomely for me and my family. Hyatt's Gold Passport program is a very good program, and I am sure that most of the hotel loyalty programs are good ones. The key is to pick the one whose hotels you think you are most likely to use. Most of these hotels also offer bonus points, etc., if you get one of their credit cards. I am not a proponent of getting too many credit cards, but one thing you can do is to get the credit card and the bonuses, and then cancel the card. Don't worry about it; you won't be the first person to do it. ☺

I was staying in Hyatt hotels when most of my travel was overseas. Once my travel became concentrated in the US, I started staying mostly in hotels that are part of the Marriott chain of properties. I have not done extensive checking, but I think the Marriott chain has more brands in their family than any other lodging chain. Here is the list of names that I could find (Marriott, JW Marriott, Renaissance, Courtyard, Residence Inn, Fairfield Inn, Marriott Conference Centers, TownPlace Suites, Spring Hill Suites, Ritz Carlton, and Marriott Vacation Club). I have personally stayed in each of the brands except

69

for the Marriott Vacation Club (their "timeshare" brand) and the JW Marriott. As one of the top elite members in their program (Marriott Rewards), I am treated to a welcoming gift (such as a bottle of wine or a plate of cheese and crackers) when I arrive at any of their hotels and they give me the best available room (no penthouse suites, though). Even though I don't travel as much as I used to, I still have a lot of points in the Marriott Rewards program – and that is after I used points to book a couple nights in Amsterdam and five nights in Paris in conjunction with our 2009 Europe trip.

There are other benefits of belonging to a hotel loyalty program, but they do vary between programs, so you should check each one before you decide which one you want to use as your main hotel program. Regardless of which one you use, get the most out of it! Most of the programs now have a lot of merchandise choices available if you would rather use your points that way.

I have one more thing to tell you about the hotel loyalty programs. Just like the airlines, most hotel programs now offer a credit card where you earn points and free nights. I receive at least one offer a week to get a credit card and I will receive lots of program points plus a free night stay after my first purchase with the card. But if you want the card and the bonus points and free night stay, just call your hotel reward program and ask them what deal they can offer you if you get their credit card. If you don't get those offers, be thankful. If you want it, it's there for the taking.

The last thing I want to discuss in this section is how you can actually make money while you are on vacation. This is not something that everyone is going to want to do, and it is not possible to do it everywhere. But if it works for you, and you want to do it, you can make some decent money for a few hours' of your time. What I am talking about is attending timeshare presentations. I go into more detail on timeshares in the next section, but the focus here is just on getting paid to look at a vacation property. Here is how it works.

Developers spend a lot of money marketing and trying to sell their vacation timeshares. One of the main ways they market them is to offer you incentives to view their property by attending a sales presentation. They will typically tell you that it is a 90-minute presentation, but some of them turn out to be 3 hour affairs (or longer!). The incentives they offer you to attend (and they hope you will then buy from them) might include cash, tickets to a dinner show or a sunset cruise. [Note: the US timeshare companies have more restrictions than those in other countries – for example, the US places will not give you cash.] When we travel to Los Cabos, Mexico, these incentives also include round-trip airport transportation – if you sign up at the airport. We have attended as many as 3 different timeshare presentations while on a four-week trip to Mexico, netting $900 cash plus round-trip airport transportation (worth another $60). So those 3 presentations put $960 into our pocket after spending about 10 total hours listening and then saying "No." As I discuss below, you may have to say "No" many times before they let you leave, but that $960 was a nice way to supplement our trip.

If you are going to sign up for one of these presentations, I suggest you push the person who originally contacts you as hard as you feel comfortable. That person has a certain amount of money that he or she is paid to bring a qualified couple into the presentation. Your goal is to get as much from that person as you can. I prefer to get all cash when I attend the presentations; the dinner voucher might not be to a restaurant I want to go to, or we might decide to go somewhere else. You can always spend the cash, but a restaurant voucher is worthless if you don't use it (and I've had a couple of them).

We did have a quite interesting thing happen after we were paid for attending a presentation. The representative there who was handling our ride back to our resort then asked us to attend a different presentation and he would match what we were just paid. We said, "Yes," and we went to his presentation and were paid again. Remember, these people – the ones who

71

sign you up – are paid to bring qualified prospects in; they really don't care if you buy or not. In fact, if you do buy, then you are not likely to sign up for any more presentations; meaning they won't get paid again. So they actually do not want you to buy. That way, you might attend a different presentation, and they can get paid again. What a racket!

As I said above, attending timeshare presentations and getting paid is not for everyone. But even if you attend only one during your vacation, you can pocket $200 -$300 spending money. Try it once and then don't do it again if it is not something you feel like doing again. Read below on how I say "No" to them. If, on the other hand, you do visit a resort and see a program that you really do like, then maybe you will want to say "Yes" instead of "No." We have purchased all four of our timeshares directly from the developer after attending one of their presentations, so we have also said "Yes" on four occasions. Two other things to keep in mind are the following:

1. The salesperson you are dealing with is paid on commission. If you are attending the presentation for the sole purpose of getting the gifts that have been promised to you (cash, show tickets, etc.), then you are not being totally honest with that salesperson. We have learned something new on each one that we have gone to, and we do want to know about the different types of timeshares that are available. We have turned down as many offers as we have gone on, and we are not going to go on one just "to get the cash."

2. You are on vacation, and you do not want to use up a lot of your precious time attending these presentations. There is typically some mental overload left over from the presentation, so it is not just the 2 or 3 hours' that you have spent there that are affected. You will feel some mental pull during the rest of that day. The point is to not feel that you should "attend as many as possible" – this is your vacation, not a money-making trip!

I want you to also remember that there are plenty of people who are reselling their ownership in most of these resorts, and you can typically buy a resale unit for 30% - 50% off the price you will pay at the resort itself. See the Reference Materials chapter for a few of the many websites where you can find timeshares that are for sale on the secondary market.

Good, bad, and ugly views of timeshares

Let me make it very clear right from the beginning that I have nothing against the timeshare industry itself and that none of mine are for sale. Now we can proceed.

I titled the section the way I did because there are many different feelings as well as misconceptions that people have about timeshares. If you see a couple who has just returned from vacation in a popular tourist area, ask them if they were "invited" to preview ownership in vacation property, aka, a "timeshare presentation." If their eyes roll or they start ranting about high-pressure sales tactics, those are sure signs that they did attend one.

Timeshares themselves are neither good nor bad. And they are certainly not ugly – in fact, most of them are extremely good looking. When you buy a timeshare you are typically purchasing the right to use a unit in a particular property for a set period of time. There are also fractional ownership properties that are deeded to you, meaning that you own it forever.

Good: Timeshares (and I will lump fractional ownership into here although some might disagree) offer you a way to vacation at nice properties in desirable locations – just like the "super rich" do. The key difference is that the very wealthy typically own their vacation home(s) outright where in a timeshare we are "sharing" the time to use the property with other timeshare owners. I like the concept. I would not want to own a vacation home full time in Cabo San Lucas, Mexico, but I do like being able to vacation there in our

73

timeshares. If you own the home or condo outright, you are responsible for all of the upkeep year-round, even for the many months that it is vacant. You do pay an annual maintenance fee with your timeshare, but that is your assurance that it will be kept up, painted, and refurbished if necessary. You also know that will it will look just as nice the second year, the third year, and so on, just as it did when you first bought it.

After a couple years of going to same place, you might decide that you want to go someplace else. If you owned your vacation home outright, you would have to find someone with a home where you wanted to go who would be willing to trade with you, or you would have to pay for renting a place. So you are essentially paying for two vacation homes – the one you own and the one you are renting. And then if you want to rent yours out, well I think you can imagine what you have to go through for that. But with a timeshare, it is relatively easy, with the emphasis on "relatively." There are numerous exchange programs and companies (see the Reference Materials chapter) who will take your timeshare week(s) and put it into their inventory of available units and locations. You then tell the exchange company when and where you want to go, and they will try to find the right match for you.

I think timeshares present a good alternative for the masses of us who cannot afford to own multi-million dollar condos on any one of the world's best beaches, ski resorts, or other paradise locations.

Bad: I alluded to high-pressure sales tactics above as one thing that probably haunts the timeshare industry more than anything else. I am **not** saying that high-pressure selling is an implicit part of that industry – people have claimed they have been the subject of high-pressure selling in many items from cars, to refrigerators, to art work, to life insurance policies. But it is a stigma that never seems to go away from the timeshare industry.

As with any large purchase, you must be knowledgeable in all the facts during the decision process when you are the buyer. Unfortunately, you do not always have them when you are looking at buying a timeshare. After you have had a beverage (and they encourage an adult beverage), the salesman will generally show you how it costs you less to vacation in your timeshare than it does if you stay in comparable hotels. You will also be told that the prices in the area are going up and this is probably your last opportunity to "own here." The sales staff is highly trained in overcoming objections, especially when your response is "We can't afford it." They have already led you down the path of showing how "you already spend more than that on your vacations right now"; so that argument is out the window. The best answer that I have used (I have also said "Yes" four times) is "We are not buying today. Thank you for your time. We have met our obligation for the 90-minute presentation, and we would like to leave now." Most times, you still don't get to leave right away – they will hand you off to someone in "Customer Service" who wants to make sure that the salesman did not offend you, etc. Actually, what they are doing is setting you up for the final pitch – either one last attempt at the timeshare itself, or a "bounce back" program where you pay for the right to come back to visit them in a year (and possibly be hassled again!). After a few more attempts to sell you something, they will sign your voucher so you can get whatever it is that was promised to you for attending the presentation.

Another "bad" side to timeshares is that you can generally find the same timeshare available online for a significant discount off the selling price at the location itself. See the Reference Materials chapter for some secondary market websites. The secondary market discount can be up to 50%, a large savings. The reason for this is that the persons now selling this timeshare have decided that they "made a mistake," "cannot afford it," or "don't want to go back there again." All I can recommend when buying a timeshare this way is to make sure you go through a reputable escrow company and have everything documented before you sign a sales agreement. You might even want to consult with an attorney.

Even if you are able to get a good deal by buying a timeshare on the secondary market, you will still be paying the same maintenance fees, and these fees can be huge. We had looked at some timeshare locations in Hawaii, and we found out that the maintenance fees were in excess of $1,000.00 per year for a single week of ownership. I was told that this is because of the extent of exterior maintenance that is required due to humidity, winds, salt, etc. A down side to buying your timeshare "sight unseen" is that you have not actually been to the property to see what it looks like. The person reselling the unit will tell you all the great things about the place, but then why is it for sale? You might save money buying a timeshare this way, but you actually will have better peace of mind buying it on site after you have visited and toured the property. Here is one area where I feel that saving a few dollars might cost you more later (when you actually visit it for the first time and start to think that you made a mistake).

Do your homework, and do not rush into the purchase of a timeshare or any other large purchase without rational thought.

Ugly: Though it was in the title of this section, I do not think there is anything ugly about timeshares. If you make good decisions about how you are going to go on vacations, then timeshares can work out well for you – we like ours and we use them every year!

That was to be the end of this section, but then we went on a timeshare presentation while in San José del Cabo, Mexico. My wife came down here for about 12 days (I was here for 29 days!), and we were invited to go to a 90-minute sales presentation at the Mayan Palace right there in San José. It took about 3 hours before the presentation reached the point where we were asked for a decision. We said, "No." It would take about three more pages for me to write out everything that happened from that point on, but essentially we were there for four and a-half hours (for what was supposed to be a 90-minute presentation) and had to go through FIVE people telling them "No" before we were finally given our "gifts" and allowed to leave. When I told the last person that one of the numerous reasons for saying "No" was the 4.5 hours' we were there even though we had been told it would be 1.5 hours, her snippy response was, "Then don't ever attend another Mayan Palace presentation!" Guess what, we never will!

So, yes; I guess there is an ugly side to timeshares, and we had just experienced it!

BONUS – Stuart's "Favorite Timeshare"

You have probably gathered by now that I think timeshares are good – maybe not for everyone, but we have enjoyed using ours. We continue to learn more about the industry and the different types of timeshares as the industry itself evolves and makes necessary changes to adapt to consumers' changing demands. Of the four timeshares that we currently own, we have three different kinds. I am going to explain those to you, and then tell you which one is my favorite.

1. **Fixed Unit/Fixed week.** We have two of these and we really like them. One of the main things that we like about the fixed week aspect of this is that we know from year to year when these are going to be, so we can make our plans well in advance. This is so important for people who have to schedule their vacation plans with employers, etc. What this does is to actually "force you" to take a vacation. I know this sounds odd, but I have known people who would not take a real vacation if they were not forced to take one. Knowing that your vacation starts on the fifth Saturday of the year removes the excuse

77

that you were not sure when you could go on vacation! This type of timeshare is also <u>fixed</u> <u>unit</u>, meaning that we have the same unit year after year. This is important because we know what it is like because it is the <u>actual</u> <u>unit</u> <u>that</u> <u>we</u> <u>purchased</u>. So there is not any guesswork about whether you will have a balcony, a view, etc. You also get to know your neighbors if they also use their unit every year. This is a great program, and we have gone back to the same resorts every year!

2. **Points.** The very first timeshare we purchased was a points-based timeshare, and we have gotten good use out of it by going to eight different resorts so far in four states (California, Nevada, Idaho, and Hawaii). This timeshare gives us a set amount of points each year to use in any of the system's resorts whenever we want to use them; for as short as a single day or up to week multiples. Each resort has a table that shows the number of points required for a given day of the week and time of the year, with the weekend days typically requiring the most points. Here is how we actually used this system for our thirtieth wedding anniversary. We drove from Boise, ID, to Lake Tahoe, NV, and stayed one night in the resort there. We drove the next morning from Lake Tahoe to Windsor, CA, in the wine country of Sonoma County. We stayed there for 5 nights. After we left Windsor we drove to Reno, NV, where we stayed in the resort for 2 nights. Then we left Reno and drove back to Boise. So we were able to stay in our system's resorts the entire trip rather than having to book hotel rooms, etc. This was a very memorable trip, especially because it was our thirtieth wedding anniversary.

3. **One-plus-One.** This timeshare is the fourth (and currently the most recent) one that we have purchased. The one-plus-one says that we "own" one week, but that we can stay an extra week (the "plus one" part) just by paying the applicable maintenance fee for that week.

Here is how it has worked for us. We own one week in a two bedroom unit for which we currently pay an annual maintenance fee of $649. We can enjoy one week in that two bedroom unit or we can actually split it into a week in a one bedroom AND a week in a studio – but that is a discussion that will take more time than allowed for in this book. If we want to double our time, we can pay "an extra maintenance fee" of $649 and now we have two weeks in that two bedroom (or two weeks in the one bedroom and two weeks in the studio). The beauty of this program is that we are not required to pay $1298 in maintenance fees each year; just the single $649 fee. We pay the second $649 only if we want to use a second week. Why wouldn't we want to double our vacation time for only $649 more – less than the price of a single airline ticket? **If there is ever a no-brainer for extending your vacation – this is it.**

I said I would tell you which one of our timeshares is our favorite one. It might be apparent to you by now that the One-plus-One that we own is our favorite one. It gives us the opportunity for extending our vacation at a fraction of the price of our airfare. When you are talking with the sales people and looking at timeshares, I highly recommend that you ask them if they offer the One-plus-One option. There are very few that do (although it seems to becoming more of the norm than it used to be), so you might have to be a little more selective to get this feature as part of your timeshare program. Even if you have to pay a small additional upfront amount to get it, get the One-plus-One option when you buy your timeshare!

Steps to planning your "ideal vacation"

Your ideal vacation will not be the same as my ideal vacation, and it will not be the same as anyone else's. That uniqueness is a part of what makes it so special and perfect – why it is <u>your</u> "ideal vacation." Here is something to keep in mind; something that others typically do not consider. Your ideal vacation does not have to be just one vacation, one trip, one adventure. In fact, <u>it</u> <u>doesn't</u> <u>even</u> <u>have</u> <u>to</u> <u>be</u> an <u>actual</u> <u>vacation</u>. Your ideal vacation could be the thoughts that you want to have, the types of places you want to go, the activities that you want to do. It could even be just the planning that you do to get ready for vacation.

I know that some will say that just thinking about a vacation is not the same as the actual vacation, and I agree with that statement. My point is that you should be able to incorporate some of the excitement of vacation into the upfront process, essentially lengthening the overall vacation time. Let's take a look at a quick example of this.

You are going to go on a 10-day cruise of the Baltic Sea (I am using this as an example because I have taken this cruise both as a paying passenger and three times as a cruise ship speaker). The cruise starts and stops in Copenhagen or Amsterdam or possibly even Stockholm. Given that you can board the ship starting at noon, you could take an overnight flight from the States into Copenhagen (for example), do a little shopping in their wonderful airport, have pastry and coffee, and then take a taxi to the wharf where you begin the embarkation process. As you go from port to port, you look at the next day's itinerary the night before and make your plans on which tour you want to go on, and what you would like to see in the city. When you go to the Activities Desk to sign up for a specific tour, you might find out that it is already sold out, so you pick another one, or just head out on your own in the city (you cannot do this in St. Petersburg, Russia, however unless you had gotten your own Russian visa prior to the trip). You continue this spontaneous travel from Denmark to Estonia to Russia to Finland to Sweden to Germany and back to Denmark where you hop in a taxi back to the airport. You will have been to all the same cities that I went to, and you will have many wonderful memories of them and even of the ship and a few of your new friends that you met onboard. You will have enjoyed your cruise and your 11-day vacation (10 days' cruising and the one day going over from the States), but it will have seemed like it was all rushed.

I suggest you consider this alternative as another way to take the same cruise. Once you have selected the cruise, book a hotel room in Copenhagen for two nights before your cruise starts. Then, go online to the cruise line website and read about the shore excursions that are offered on your cruise. You do not have to take one in each port, and you also have to determine which ones and how many of them will fit into your budget. Even though Tallinn, Estonia, might be your first stop, you can just walk through the town on our own and have a very enjoyable time. After you have selected the possible excursions, do a little more research on them. Would you rather have more time on the guided tour, or would you rather have some free time because you want to go exploring the flower gardens or the amber factories on your own? Write down all the excursions, and then put an asterisk besides the ones that are your current favorites. Put the list down for a couple of days. When you look at this list again, go back over your selections and see if they still are your favorites. If so, go online and reserve them. Most of them do have limited capacity and they do sell out – don't wait until you are onboard the ship and then find out that the only available tour is one that no one else wants to go on (which is why it is the only one still available). You might even rent a video or do some online research about the places you are going to see so that you begin each tour with a small amount of knowledge.

Since you are flying over to Copenhagen a couple days early, you will be able to go straight to your hotel right from the airport. Even though you might be tempted to take a "short nap," change into comfortable walking clothes and shoes and head out for a short walking tour of the downtown area. Stop in one of the many local cafés and enjoy a lunch and your choice of beverage. It is important to stay very busy that first day and to avoid the temptation to take a nap in the hotel room. By staying up and moving about, you will be really ready for a good night's sleep when evening rolls around and you will be able to get your body in tune with local time. It would be terrible for you to get on the cruise and be tired during the days when you are in port at some very exciting destinations. You should awake fully refreshed your next day in Copenhagen, and you then expand your sightseeing activities to include art museums, shopping, etc. (My brother took a taxi to the Harley-Davidson dealership to buy a shirt with Copenhagen on it).

Once the third day gets there, your body will be in sync as if you had been there for a long time. You will be refreshed when you board the ship, and you will be able to fully enjoy all the pre-sailing and post-sailing activities. Plus, your shore excursions will be much more enjoyable because you have researched them and you will be going on the ones that you want to go on. When you finally get back to Copenhagen, take a taxi to the airport and fly home. I guarantee that this vacation will be much, much more pleasurable than the first one I described.

Gee, Stuart, that's fine if you are going on a cruise. We are only planning a vacation to "the coast." What can we do to turn that into your idea of an "ideal vacation"? The same ideas will work for this trip as they do for the cruise. You might not have to book extra time, although you might consider adding a day or two (or more) to start or end the vacation with a stay at a spa resort. Have yourself pampered where your only job is to relax, enjoy a soothing massage, and just feel comfortable. If going to a spa is not something you want to do (you should try it, however), then use those extra days to visit some historic sites or artist communities. Do something that you would not ordinarily do – those are the activities that you will remember and that you will comment on as to why that trip was ideal and memorable.

Here is a summary of my checklist of things you can do before you go on any vacation; these are some things that can help turn an "ordinary" vacation into an "ideal" one.

- Think about more than one vacation at a time. When you have more than one vacation planned in advance, you are able to enjoy the planning process much more. You are also not forcing yourself to do everything that you want to do "on vacation" in just one vacation. You are able to include more of your favorite activities into your overall planning because you are planning more than one vacation at a time.

- Why do you want to go where you want to go? Are there specific places you want to visit while you are there, or are you going because you "always wanted to go there"? Write down your reasons; you might find that a month later there is a different location that will satisfy your reasons more than your original place. If you want to go to Paris, France, in June – remember that the French Open (tennis) is there for the first two weeks of June. So if tennis is not your thing, and you want to avoid the crowds associated with that major event, pick a different time of the year to visit Paris. However, if you do enjoy tennis as well as the excitement that surrounds one of tennis' four grand slam events, then plan far ahead to get your travel and accommodations.

- If you have been to your vacation spot before, write down what you really liked about it and what you would like to do again. Also write down what was the least enjoyable about that place. Why was it not enjoyable for you? Was the weather not what you had expected? Did you or someone else get sick or have a bad time for some other reason? We went to the island of Kauai in Hawaii one year in March. We had not even left the main terminal before my wife's allergies kicked in full force. Despite her taking her medications and inhalers, it was a miserable trip for her. It's called the "Garden Isle" for a reason – it is definitely green and lush. But

83

that is no longer a plus for us, and it might not be a plus for you if you are highly sensitive to all the plants that can irritate your allergies.

- Somewhat like the previous step, write down the things that you have enjoyed about previous vacations even if you are not planning on going back to the same places. Also write down what you didn't like about any of your vacations. Then think about why some were good activities, and why some were not. As you consider going to different places, do some quick research to see if the enjoyable activities are available there. Likewise, try to determine if the things that you did not like might occur there (bad weather, lots of bugs and flying insects, etc.). You might end up eliminating what you thought would be a great place to visit – but it is better to eliminate that spot <u>before</u> you go than to regret it once you arrived there.

- If you are going to a place where you have cooking facilities, take along some of your favorite spices and seasonings, as well as a few simple-to-prepare food items (tea bags, coffee and filters, oatmeal, microwave popcorn, etc.). Also take along some re-sealable storage bags. Having a few familiar items with you will make the transition from home to vacation a little easier. Some people like to eat every meal out when they are on vacation; others like to have some food items available in case they want to stay in for breakfast, or have just a quick bite for lunch. If you are not sure if the place you are staying has any kitchen facilities (it could be a full-size kitchen or a small kitchenette with a microwave oven and a mini-refrigerator), contact the place and ask them.

- We have a small pocket-size notebook that we have labeled "Travel." We take that with us everywhere so we can write down things as we think of them. There are some things that we want to have with us no matter where we go, and then there are other items that are specific to a particular location or type of vacation. We have separate pages for them, and we keep track of what we want to take along. We sometimes make a conscious decision to not take one of the items with us, but at least we think about them before we go. We also update each list as we are on vacation because one or two things might be taken off the list as new items are being added. For example, we include our reef shoes and snorkel gear when we are going to a beach area, but we don't take them if we are going somewhere else. We take a night light with us everywhere to plug into a bathroom socket. It will take a while until your lists become really useful to you; but start making them now while it is fresh in your mind.

- Speaking of lists, you also want to have a list of things to do <u>before</u> you leave on vacation. Are you going to stop the newspapers, and are you going to have someone take in your mail for you? Have you given your houseplants a thorough watering before you leave? Who knows your itinerary and can be a contact point in case there is an emergency at your house while you are gone (broken water line, etc.)? Have you reset your thermostat to a comfortable, yet reasonable temperature while you are gone? It might be 95 degrees outside, but the inside of your house does not need to be 72 degrees for the entire time you are gone. Even pushing it up to 75 will reduce your electricity bill, and the house will not be uncomfortable when you return. If you have pets, you will need to make arrangements for their boarding well in advance of your departure (unless they are going with you, of course). One thing that is very easy to forget is to pay your monthly bills in advance so you do not arrive home and find out that you forgot to pay them, and now you will be facing late fees. If you don't want to mail them too early, write out the checks and put them in the stamped envelope, and then write the mailing date in pencil in the lower left corner of the envelope. Ask a trusted friend to mail them for you on the date you have written on each envelope. Another way to pay your bills while you are on vacation is to schedule online payments from your checking account.

- Whenever you are on vacation, pick up the take-out menus at the restaurants that you really like. These can be casual lunch places or higher-end dining establishments. Many of them might not have a menu that you can take with you, so find something to take along as a reminder of the place. Then when you are planning your next vacation to that location you can look at the menu or whatever else you brought home, and plan with anticipation your upcoming meal there. Even if you do not return to the same vacation spot, you are now assembling a list of the types of restaurants that you like. You can use this listing to help you select one in your new vacation spot, or it can be a reference for a friend of yours who is traveling there. I know that I love getting a recommendation for a good restaurant; chances are that your friends will too.

I am sure that you will be able to come up with more things to do to plan your ideal vacation. If you wish to share them with me _and_ with others, please send them to me at stuart.a.gustafson.@gmailcom. Thank you, and I certainly do hope that enjoy your next vacation, and all the ones after that!

9 - FOUR PEOPLE you should know well, and vice versa

This chapter could very well be considered the most controversial chapter in the entire book. I hope it is because that means that the readers are discussing the book's contents and evaluating which pieces are more important or more relevant. Frankly, I felt that all of the chapters are critical to the development of the book and its contribution to your own successful retirement. And I hope that you feel the same way.

The four people I discuss in the chapter are very important to a successful retirement in many different ways. Each one of these persons has their own skills which have been acquired through education and then continually honed through additional courses and study programs. While each one of these people may have an advanced degree (or maybe even more than one), it is not the diplomas on the wall that are going to help you in retirement; it is the knowledge and advice that each person provides to you that is important. You might be able to find the answer to a legal question by posting to an online newsgroup or looking for the answer in a search engine. But none of those answers or advice will compare to the competent legal advice that you will receive from a qualified person who can address your situation. Not only is it necessary for you to know these people, but they must also know you, your situation, and your condition. Okay, it's time to get off the soap box and to introduce you to four very important people.

Doctor – I sincerely hope that no MDs come after me because I am gong to include many "doctors" in this category. As you enter the retirement phase it becomes even more important for you to have regular visits with your doctor. When I say doctor, I mean a professional medical person who can diagnose and address certain medical and physical parts of your life. Your retirement will be much more enjoyable when you take care of your health – both pro-active and preventative.

I used to say that it "was important" as you get older to have regular (at least once a year) visits with your "general health doctor." You know what? It is more than important; it's a prerequisite for a healthy retirement. These regular visits should include a thorough physical examination as well as specialized examinations that check for forms of cancer or other problems that need monitoring. Pay special attention to the risk factors that run in your family (diabetes, heart disease, breast cancer, etc.). Don't be afraid to have the following examinations as they are appropriate for you: colonoscopy, breast examination, Pap smear, diabetes tests, prostate examination, etc. Your doctor will tell you which ones you should have on an annual basis, and which are ones you should have every two years, every three years, etc. Listen to him or her, and pay special attention to the results of those examinations. Discovering that you have cancer is not a happy time, but many cancers can be treated and eliminated when they are diagnosed in the early stages. If you don't have your regular examinations, you might not catch this early on, and we all know what happens after that.

My eldest brother (just about to turn 67) was told that a small polyp that was removed during a routine colonoscopy was cancerous, so he was scheduled for exploratory surgery. He had this surgery while my son and I were in San Diego for the US Open Tournament a few years ago. He and his wife were justifiably concerned. What a relief we all felt when he was told that the part of the colon they removed (where the removed polyp had been) had no signs of cancer. He has no follow-ups at all – no treatments or anything else. His routine exams found something that could have become a major problem if not located and removed.

Oral hygiene is an area that is easily overlooked, yet it is so essential to your long-term health (and the enjoyment of your retirement). Most people think they should have their teeth cleaned every six months by a dental hygienist. While there, they will typically have an examination by the dentist. Most people know that the "every six months" program is because that is what most insurance companies will allow and pay for under their coverage. But what they don't know is that it used to be once a year. According to an article by Trisha O'Hehir on the Dental Economics website (http://www.dentaleconomics.com/display_article/171263/56/ARCHI/none/Colum/The-mystery-of-recall-intervals?),

> It wasn't research that changed the yearly check-up to six months — it was Bucky Beaver. Ipana toothpaste commercials featured Bucky Beaver, telling us to "...use Ipana toothpaste and see the dentist twice a year." This seems to have replaced the previous tradition of yearly visits, especially for children.

So you want to add your dentist and his professional staff to your list of "doctors" to visit on a regular basis. I don't know the numbers, but I have read that gum disease, gingivitis, etc., are leading causes of oral cancer. Have your regular check-ups to ensure that you are not caught by surprise when you visit your doctor or dentist and he or she tells you that you have some form of oral cancer. Or worse, that it has spread to other parts of your body.

Another doctor you want to visit regularly is your "eye doctor." There are three primary types of doctors in this category according to the online source *Web*MD.com (http://www.webmd.com/eye-health/choosing-eye-doctor). Here are quotes from that source. "Ophthalmologists are eye doctors that specialize in the medical and surgical care of the eyes and visual system, and also the prevention of eye disease and injury. They can be either doctors of medicine (MD) or doctors of osteopathy (DO)." "Optometrists are eye doctors of optometry (OD). They are trained to examine, diagnose, treat, and manage some diseases and disorders of the eye and visual system." "Opticians are eye healthcare professionals who work with ophthalmologists and optometrists to provide vision services related to the diagnosis and treatment of vision problems and eye disease." According to WebMD, opticians are not required to have an advanced degree or even a four-year degree. You want to <u>schedule an annual visit with your ophthalmologist or optometrist</u> who will check your vision, test for glaucoma and other potential diseases of the eye, and give you a prescription for glasses or contact lenses. The health of your eyes is every bit as important as the health of the rest of your body. What is the point of going on that dream vacation if you can't see well because you don't have an updated prescription for your glasses, or you have cataracts that have not yet been diagnosed?

I suggest that you visit the "Health" websites that are listed in the Reference Materials chapter. The Travelers Vaccines website is also a good one to check out if you are going to be traveling outside the United States. You can find out which vaccinations are needed or recommended for which countries, and you also find out how often you should have then renewed or get a booster shot. NOTE: this website is provided by a pharmaceuticals firm, rather than by a governmental agency. As with all health concerns, check with your own medical professional before making any decisions.

Lawyer – Visiting with a lawyer on an annual basis is typically not a requirement when you enter retirement. But the reason you must know this person well, and vice versa, is because it is the lawyer who is going to write your will, your living will, and your durable power of attorney that we discussed earlier. Your lawyer will have attended law school, will typically have a JD degree, and will have passed the bar examination in your state (or be allowed to practice in your state through a reciprocity arrangement with another state). He or she might have a paralegal or a junior attorney work on your documents, but it will be your attorney who will do the final review of these documents and go over them with you.

The development of these critical documents is not the only reason for "having an attorney." A situation might arise where you want to retain the services of an attorney, or even just consult with one. This situation might result from some injury to you (or others); you feel that you have been wronged somehow; someone is bringing legal action against you, or it might even be a potential business opportunity you want to consider. By having an attorney you are comfortable working with, and one who knows a little about you and your situation, you can go to this person as your first point of contact. He or she might not be a specialist in the area that you need at this time, but your attorney will be able to direct you to one, possibly even in the same firm.

Working with an attorney in the same firm as your attorney has advantages – no "new client forms" to complete; already set up in their billing system; access to an attorney you might not otherwise be able to see; heightened interest from this new attorney so you don't take your business to another firm. If you don't already have an attorney, or if you want to find a different one, talk to some of your friends and tell them you are looking for an attorney to handle some of your personal and business needs. Do they have one they feel very comfortable with? Would they recommend that you go to the same attorney as they do? Would they introduce you to him or her? I am a fan of advertising, but I don't think you should select an attorney who does a lot of advertising on the television, in the newspapers, or on the covers of telephone books.

I have recently become a fan of the Certified Elder Law Attorney designation. As I discussed earlier, this small subset of attorneys specializes in legal matters pertaining to "the elderly" – an age that seems to include more of us every year! There is a link to the National Elder Law Foundation in the Reference Materials chapter. These CELAs can also show you ways to shelter money in legal yet little-known vehicles so that you (or your parents) will have the assets – as well as the access to them – when those assets are needed most.

91

You might have to pay a little more for their services as they draft the specialty documents for you; your long-term savings and peace of mind should definitely outweigh those costs.

Tax Accountant – Most people don't think that they need a tax accountant because "Our finances are not that complicated. We can take our taxes to [*any one of dozens of tax preparation firms*] and have them done for a lot less." That might work for many people, and I have nothing against the tax preparation firms. But I think this is a situation where you can hurt yourself in the long round by pinching pennies in the short run. Our tax accountant, a Certified Public Accountant (CPA), charges a very high hourly rate. So we make sure that we get full use of his time and attention when we are in his office. I know we have saved more than he has charged us – or at least I think we have. The key point is that I know we are making good decisions regarding taxes and other financial activities because of our working with him.

The income tax laws are always changing, and it is his job to keep up with them; it is not ours. My wife is an accountant by education and trade, but she has no interest in trying to stay current in tax laws. One specific example where our CPA has helped us is in how to treat my book writing business as a business entity. I have been able to legally (and I cannot stress that concept enough!) write off certain expenses because they were directly related to writing books, etc. So I have been able to actually make money just by going to certain places to gather information for my books and then to write them. He has also counseled us in determining when to make a certain financial transaction so we are able to incur a minimal tax impact on that transaction. The net gain on that one piece of advice alone will pay for his services for many years into the future. We use the services of our tax accountant not just in the preparation of our taxes, but also in planning when and how we structure certain financial aspects of our life. If you do not have a tax accountant who is working with you and <u>saving you money</u>, then I suggest that you find one who will.

Financial Consultant – This fourth person you need to know and work with is not easy to describe because he or she does not fit into a nice simple description or definition. There are financial consultants who have attained various industry certifications, and then there are the consultants who do not have the letters behind their names. Here are a few of the designations that are out there: Accredited Asset Management Specialist (AAMS), Certified Financial Planner (CFP), Chartered Financial Analyst (CFA), Certified Fund Specialist (CFS), Chartered Financial Consultant (ChFC), Chartered Investment Counselor (CIC), Certified Investment Management Analyst (CIMA), Chartered Market Technician (CMT), Certified Public Accountant (CPA), Personal Financial Specialist (PFS), Chartered Life Underwriter (CLU).

While a particular designation indications the completion of a particular course of study, the lack of a designation does not mean that the person is not qualified to provide <u>you</u> with financial consultation. As with any professional relationship (medical, legal, or financial) you must feel extremely comfortable with this person and with the advice that you are receiving. After all, the financial consultant is talking about <u>your money</u> – that should be enough reason for you to be completely engaged! In order for your relationship with a financial consultant to be the most beneficial, you have to be open and candid with him or her. What is that you want from the relationship? Do you want general advice that gives you basic education about asset allocation; do you want specific stock tips; do you want this person to actually select the vehicles where your money is going to be invested? There is no one single scenario that works for everyone, and so that is why you have to develop an ongoing relationship with your financial consultant. It cannot be just a one-time conversation.

An interesting point is that you might have more than one financial consultant. Why would you want to do this? The answer is that each financial consultant typically has an area of expertise – meaning that he or she knows a lot about a few things, but then there are a lot of things that that he or she is not that knowledgeable in. Maybe you have been working with a financial consultant for ten years and he has always given you great advice in traditional equity investments (stocks, bonds, mutual funds, etc.). But now you have been given an opportunity where you are considering making a significant investment into a tax-sheltered real estate consortium. Your financial consultant – even though he will do his best to give you the best advice that he can – might not be the person best qualified to give you financial advice in this situation. He may be able to recommend another consultant who can help you; or perhaps your attorney or tax accountant can give you advice or a recommendation.

Another situation is that maybe your savings and investment picture has changed – for better or for worse. Maybe you have just received an inheritance and you want to shift some of your assets from income to growth vehicles. Or, perhaps you have had to pull out a significant portion of your savings to pay for a catastrophic illness or help out a family member. You want a financial consultant who can help you make the best decisions for you in these situations. The key is that you have to feel comfortable in working with the professionals who are going to do the best job for you. It is your money, and you have an obligation to yourself (and to your family) to make the best decisions that achieve the financial goals that are right for you.

10 - Reference Materials

NOTICE: *These names and web links are given for informational reference only. I have not requested, nor have I received, any benefits from the businesses listed below. The ones that I recommend are there because I have used them and I do like them! As in all affairs, you are urged to seek competent professional advice in any business transactions.*

RETIREMENT ACTIVITIES:

Here is the format I have used for my "Retirement Activities" list. Feel free to copy and modify this table so it best works for you.

#	Activity	When/How long	Done	When
18	Attend one of the 4 PGA slam events (Masters, US Open, British Open, PGA Championship)	1 week	YES	US Open 6/08
1	Camp in Idaho – several 1-2 week trips to different spots in Idaho	Various times in year	YES	various
2	Re-gain "semi-fluency" in Russian	Ongoing		
3	"Highlights" tour of Europe	4 weeks		May 2009
4	"Drive Idaho" either in car or motor home	1 month		
5	Paris, France – rent a flat for 2 months in the city; side trips to countryside; live the French life	2 months –	YES	May - July 2014

HEALTH SITES:

I've said it before but I will say it again, "Your retirement will be much more enjoyable when you take care of your health – both pro-active and preventative." Here are just a few sites that have excellent information.

American Medical Association – http://www.ama-assn.org.

American Dental Association – http://www.ada.org.

American Optometric Association – http://www.aoa.org.

WebMD – "Better information. Better health." http://webmd.com.

Traveler's Health Information from the Center for Disease Control and Prevention – http://wwwn.cdc.gov/travel/default.aspx.

Travelers Vaccines - http://www.travelersvaccines.com/En. - Has valuable information on vaccinations for overseas travel. [NOTE: this website is maintained by a pharmaceuticals company, not a governmental agency]

MY BOOKS:

The best place to find my books is on my website stuartgustafson.com. You will find links to online sellers as well as which ones can be purchased directly from me.

OTHER BOOKS I HIGHLY RECOMMEND:

Second Acts by Stephen M. Pollan and Mark Levine. "Creating the life you really want, building the career you truly desire."

The Book of Virtues edited, with commentary, by William J. Bennett. "A Treasury of Great Moral Stories."

The Essential BUFFETT by Robert G. Hagstrom. "Timeless Principles for the New Economy."

The Tipping Point by Malcom Gladwell. "How Little Things can Make a Big Difference."

Blink by Malcolm Gladwell. "The Power of Thinking Without Thinking."

The World is Flat by Thomas L. Friedman. "A Brief History of the Twenty-first Century."

FINANCIAL SITES:

The US Government publishes per diem rates for allowable expenses in both the Continental US (CONUS) and Outside the Continental US, including Alaska and Hawaii (OCONUS). Check with your tax advisor for the applicability of these rates in your situation. CONUS rates are in IRS Publication 1542 in PDF format (http://www.irs.gov/pub/irs-pdf/p1542.pdf). OCONUS rates are available in various formats, including Microsoft Excel (http://www.state.gov/www/perdiems/index.html).

Here is a website that lists foreign exchange rates, and it has a calculator for exchanging X amount of one currency for Y amount in another currency. I use this website, and find it quite handy (http://finance.yahoo.com/currency).

U.S. Savings Bonds - http://www.savingsbonds.gov. This site has all the information you would ever want about Savings Bonds, including Savings Bonds Rates and the Savings Bond Calculator. The latter is a handy tool that I have used; I recommend using it!

Social Security (US only)

Main website – www.ssa.gov.

Calculate your benefits – www.ssa.gov/planners/calculators.htm.

To request your personal Social Security statement – www.ssa.gov/mystatement/.

Common Social Security forms – www.ssa.gov/online/.

LEGAL "STUFF":

Nolo Press – www.nolopress.com. They are a wealth of information for legal books, forms, and software (although <u>not</u> a substitute for your attorney). "Since 1971, Nolo's goal has been simple: To make America's legal system accessible to everyone. With hundreds of top quality, plain-English legal products, we've helped make that happen."

National Elder Law Foundation – www.nelf.org. This is <u>the</u> legal organization that focuses on Elder Law, "the legal practice of counseling and representing older persons and their representatives about the legal aspects of health and long-term care planning, public benefits, surrogate decision-making, older persons' legal capacity, the conservation, disposition and administration of older persons' estates and the implementation of their decisions concerning such matters, giving due consideration to the applicable tax consequences of the action, or the need for more sophisticated tax expertise." **Use them!** This is emphasized in Chapters 7 & 9.

Information about legal issues – www.lawyers.com. The heading on this web page is "Find an Attorney." I don't think this is the <u>best</u> way to find an attorney. (that subject is covered in Chapter 9). This website does, however, have some good stuff under "Things to know before you ...." There's no harm in looking at it. More input is better than no information at all.

TRAVEL/VACATION:

US Passport information:

http://travel.state.gov/passport is the main website

You will find numerous links on the main passport page for application procedures, where you can apply for a passport, processing times, etc.

Canadian Passport information (French and English versions available):

http://www.pptc.gc.ca is the main website

United States Embassies, etc., - http://www.usembassy.gov. This site has the sites of US Embassies, Consulates, and Diplomatic Missions around the world.

Just a few of the websites for last-minute travel deals:
www.lastminutetravel.com.
www.11thhourvacations.com.
www.last-minute.travelzoo.com.
www.us.lastminute.com.
www.hotwire.com.

Some of the numerous timeshare exchange companies:
Holiday Systems International – www.holidaysystems.com.
Interval International – www.intervalworld.com.
RCI – www.rci.com.
Trading Places International – www.tradingplaces.com .
San Francisco Exchange (higher-end resorts) – www.sfx-resorts.com.

For great tours in Europe, I recommend "Rick Steves – Europe Through the Back Door" – www.ricksteves.com. My wife and I are taking a 21-day "Best of Europe" tour in May 2009. Even if you don't take any tours, the website contains excellent travel help and guides (and their luggage is wonderful and lightweight – we have it and we have used it on numerous trips!). We are also planning on a 13-day trip in 2011 through the villages and vineyards of Eastern France.

Elderhostel® – America's first and the world's largest educational travel organization for adults 55 and over. They offer unique educational experiences, infused with the spirit of camaraderie and adventure, which enrich and enhance the lives of its participants. Even if you don't go on one of their "programs," order their free catalog just to get an idea of interesting places to go and things to do – in your own state, or half way around the world – http://www.elderhostel.org.

Secondary markets for timeshares (buying and selling):
www.redweek.com.
www.vacationcredits.com.
www.timeshareliquidationservice.com.
www.sellmytimesharenow.com.
www.alltimeshare.com.

Some good tips about traveling in another country - http://www.gestbiz.com/articles/Article/Legal-Tips-When-Traveling-Overseas/17660.

"Seat Guru" is the website for "The ultimate source for airline seating, in-flight amenities and airline information." I use this site and I highly recommend it – www.seatguru.com. A recent example is that Untied has changed the configuration of their international 747's – SeatGuru has the up-to-date information that my "seat booklet" didn't have.

Major US airlines:
Alaska Airlines – www.alaskaair.com.
America West – www.americawest.com.
American – www.aa.com.
Delta Airlines – www.delta.com.
Southwest Airlines – www.iflyswa.com.
United Airlines – www.united.com.

Other airlines serving US airports:

AeroMexico – www.aeromexico.com.

Air Canada – www.aircanada.ca.

Air France – www.airfrance.fr.

Alitalia – www.alitalia.it.

Lufthansa Airlines – www.lufthansa.com.

Mexicana Airlines – www.mexicana.com.

Scandinavian Airlines System (SAS) – www.scandinavian.net.

Swissair – www.swissair.com.

Virgin Atlantic – www.virgin-atlantic.com.

"Airline Partner" programs (typically your flights on any of the airlines in a given program will earn miles for you in your specific airline program, if it is part of that partner program; most also have hotel and car rental partners that can earn you points in your airline program):

Star Alliance (this is just a few of the 20+ airline members) – www.staralliance.com.

United Airlines

Lufthansa Airlines

SAS

Singapore Airlines

Air Canada

Air New Zealand

Delta Airlines SkyMiles® program (some of the 20 participating airlines)

Delta Airlines

Alaska Airlines

Continental Airlines

Northwest Airlines

Singapore Airlines

Virgin Atlantic Airways

American Airlines AAdvantage® program (some of the 20+
participating airlines)

American Airlines

Alaska Airlines

British Airways

Cathay Pacific

Hawaiian Airlines

Mexicana

Qantas Airways

Hotels and resorts in the US:

Marriott Hotels and Resorts – www.marriott.com.

Hilton Hotels – www.hilton.com.

Hyatt Hotels and Resorts – www.hyatt.com.

Starwood Hotels & Resorts (Westin, Sheraton, Le Meridien, St. Regis,
and others) – www.starwood.com.

Crowne Plaza Hotels & Resorts – www.crowneplaza.com.

Best Western Hotels – www.bestwestern.com.

11 - THANK YOU

I do want to sincerely <u>thank</u> <u>you</u> for buying and reading ***Mastering "The Art of Retirement."*** I trust that you learned a lot more about yourself as well as many things that you can put to good use as you plan for and enjoy your own retirement. Please tell your friends and family what you are using from this book to enhance your preparation <u>and</u> your retirement. Also, please send an email to me telling me about your experiences and what you have found most helpful in the book. I would love to be able to share with others how you benefited from the book with – and I am confident that they would also appreciate them.

Send your emails to stuart.a.gustafson@gmail.com.

Happy Retirement!

12 - About the Author

Stuart Gustafson was fortunate to be able to retire at age 59. He loves to travel, and he channels this passion, as well as his vast knowledge of travel, into mystery novels set in exciting locations. The holder of the U.S. Registered Trademark *America's International Travel Expert®*, he has visited over 50 countries, over 100 cruise ports, and has his Million-Mile Flier card from a major U.S.-based airline. He's frequently invited by the cruise lines to sail with them to exotic locations to speak about the art, the history, and the culture of the cruise destinations. He makes the talks come alive, and thus the guests are more knowledgeable and comfortable as they venture out to new places.

With a BA in Mathematics and an MBA, Stuart worked in high technology fields for twenty-nine years in Southern California and in Idaho before taking early retirement in 2007. Since then, he's been able to spend more time writing and, of course, traveling. He even took his then 90-year-old mother on a 14-day New Zealand cruise, her last major trip. He and his wife Darlene spend two to four weeks each year in Cabo San Lucas and San José del Cabo, at the very tip of Mexico's Baja California peninsula, a delightful location that served as the basis for his Amazon Best Selling and Top Rated debut mystery novel *Missing in Mexico*.

He and his wife, and their rescue dog, live in Boise, Idaho, when they're not traveling somewhere. Find out more about Stuart's books as well as travel information and tips at www.StuartGustafson.com.

www.ingramcontent.com/pod-product-compliance
Lightning Source LLC
Chambersburg PA
CBHW020923180526
45163CB00007B/2865